The Prisons We Deserve

The Prisons We Deserve

Andrew Coyle

HarperCollins*Publishers*

HarperCollins*Publishers*
77–85 Fulham Palace Road, London W6 8JB

First published in Great Britain
in 1994 by HarperCollins*Publishers*

1   3   5   7   9   10   8   6   4   2

A catalogue record for this book is
available from the British Library

ISBN 0 00 627654-7

Typeset by Harper Phototypesetters Limited,
Northampton, England
Printed and bound in Great Britain by
HarperCollinsManufacturing Glasgow

Contents

ONE

Introduction

One of the most frequent opening exchanges at a social gathering where people do not know each other is surely, 'And what do you do for a living?' My answer, 'I'm a prison governor', usually elicits more than a little interest. Once the questioner has recovered from initial surprise, the next response for years was, 'You look too young to be a prison governor.' I get that response less and less nowadays. The alternative was, and often still is, 'You don't look like a prison governor.' What should a prison governor look like?

Invariably people want to take the opportunity to explore the closed world of the prison. 'I hope you don't mind me asking, but what does a prison governor do?' Or 'Tell me, what is prison really like?' The answer to these questions is the subject matter of this book.

Over the years I have had the opportunity to visit prisons in many parts of the world: in the Caribbean, in North America, in Asia, in Africa and across Europe. Some of them have been new prisons, well-built with good security and fully equipped. Others have been old, squalid relics from a previous age. Yet basically prisons are the same the world over. They are buildings in which one group of human beings deprives another group of human beings of their liberty. They may do it humanely and with care or they may do it brutally and without feeling, but in each case the principle remains the same.

There are certain basic requirements of humanity which are not negotiable when it comes to running prisons. These include prohibition against torture, the obligation to feed prisoners, to give them access to medical care, to allow them to observe their religion, to allow their families to visit. These and other universal norms and guidelines are contained in various United Nations documents relating to the treatment of prisoners, such as the Basic Principles for the Treatment of Prisoners, and in regional provisions, such as the European Prison Rules.

The universal norms are necessarily general rather than specific in content. Day-to-day conditions in prisons vary greatly from country to country. That is not only inevitable, it is proper. Prisons reflect the societies in which they exist. A convicted prisoner in the former Soviet Union is likely to be held in a labour colony, which will be in effect a large factory with hostel-type accommodation attached. A high security prisoner in the United States is likely to be kept in a cell on his own and to be shackled whenever he moves out of that cell for whatever reason. Prisoners in some countries will be allowed to visit their families at regular intervals. In many countries families are allowed to come into the prison to spend several days at a time with the prisoner in a specially designated area. In other countries prisoners are permitted to have very little contact with their families.

The practice of locking up human beings in conditions of captivity challenges some of the basic principles of humanity. For that reason one should be prepared to ask first-order questions. Why do we have prisons? What are they meant to achieve? Does everyone who is in prison now have to be there? Are there other ways of dealing with people who break the accepted norms of society? How are prisons run? Could they be run better?

Imprisonment as a punishment in its own right is a relatively new phenomenon which has been developed over the last 200 years. Imprisonment and the structures which support it have developed in a very pragmatic manner with little coherence. Rationalization and justification have usually come after the event. It was some time after courts began to use imprisonment as a direct sentence that theorists began to discuss the purpose of imprisonment and the aims of the prison. As a consequence, many of the arguments for the use of imprisonment are based on a justification of what is already being done rather than on principle.

In a perverse fashion, this has hed to an increased belief in the need for imprisonment. This has reached the stage where we talk without thinking about alternatives to imprisonment. It is as if imprisonment were the first option of the sentencer and other forms of judicial penalty only to be used when imprisonment is not appropriate.

This notion has been fuelled in recent years by various players in the debate about crime, its causes and its effects. Not least has been the influence of some sections of the media who have led the public in its ambivalence about the way we use imprisonment as a punishment. On the one hand there is a cry for more extensive use of imprisonment and for longer prison sentences. On the other hand there is criticism of the overcrowded prison system and its poor conditions and of the fact that it is clearly a signal failure as a means of preventing future criminality.

Such vagueness about the purpose of imprisonment and its use did not create any major difficulty, at least in practice, while the system was under no great pressure. It could muddle along, with few questions being asked other than by a handful of concerned groups. Few people interested themselves in what went on behind the high walls of our prisons. Statisticians might earn a living by churning out figures describing rates of imprisonment per hundred thousand of the population and rates of recidivism among released prisoners, but little attention was paid to them.

This lack of clarity about the purpose of imprisonment and the reason for depriving certain members of the community of their liberty was only likely to be challenged when prison systems came under significant pressure for one reason or another. And this was indeed what happened on an international scale. One such pressure was overcrowding, with prisons which had been built to hold 100 prisoners being asked to contain 200 and prisons with places for 1,000 prisoners having to squeeze in 2,000 or more. Another pressure came from the increasing violence which pervaded many prisons across the world, violence of prisoner on guard, guard on prisoner and prisoner on prisoner.

All of this in turn led to pressure on human rights groups, lawyers and eventually the judiciary to take an interest in what was going on in prisons. In due course academics began to address themselves in a co-ordinated way to questions about the purpose and use of imprisonment. Managers of prison systems and of prisons were forced to look at how the system was organized.

Many of these pressures and consequent changes have occurred during the last twenty years. My personal experience of prisons covers broadly the same period. This is a parallel which has led me to attempt to chart some of these changes in prisons and in prison systems. It is appropriate that I should do so from a personal perspective which brings to the analysis a blend of academic knowledge and of practical experience.

One of my first sensations on joining the prison service was of lack of direction. There was no obvious point of reference for this new world which I had entered. In common with most reasonably well-informed citizens I had been aware of the existence of a prison system. From time to time I read about it in the press in a detached sort of a way. More than that I did not know.

I did not join the prison service out of a burning sense of vocation. I wanted the opportunity to work with people and to be of some public service. The advertisement in the press for 'Assistant Governors' in the prison service in January 1973 was vague enough to excite my interest. After the initial application the process moved inexorably on until I was offered an appointment in the Scottish Prison Service at Edinburgh Prison in September 1973.

From the outset I felt a personal need to place the prison system and the whole notion of imprisonment within a context. I soon found that there were so many obvious inconsistencies in how prisons operated and uncertainties about their purpose. One was continually reminded of the tourist who asked the local farmer how to get to a particular spot. 'Well,' came the answer, 'I certainly wouldn't start from here.' It was necessary to go back to the beginning, to learn something about the development of punishment in our society and how imprisonment came to have such a central role in the expression of that punishment.

I set myself the task of learning about the history of imprisonment in the hope of gaining some idea about how imprisonment, if it was thought to be necessary in the future, might be better organized. In the course of this research I learned something of the philosophy of punishment and how a new breed of academics called criminologists had developed a whole set of arguments about people who were convicted of breaking the law and how another set of academics called penologists, who were half-brothers to the criminologists, now spent their time discussing models of punishment.

But my main learning over the last twenty years has not come from books. It has come from a hard-won experience which has changed my outlook on the world. No one who has not been a prisoner can really know what prison is like. But to have worked for half a professional lifetime in prison does leave one with a degree of understanding of the subject.

This book reflects that personal experience. The main subjects which are discussed are placed in the context of my own professional life. I have worked with remand prisoners, prisoners serving short sentences and those serving very long sentences. I have worked with women prisoners and with young offenders. I have worked at the centre of the organization. I have taken a special interest in the staff who work in prisons. Each of these groups are integral players in the world of the prison.

Prisons are usually only in the news when things within them are going wrong. They have been much in the news over the last twenty years. There have been many positive advances in the prison systems of the United Kingdom during that period but these have been little reported. Instead, the public has been fed a steady diet of riots, hostage-takings, escapes and industrial action. It took the worst riot in the history of prisons in Great Britain to lead to the most far-reaching analysis of the prison system which has ever been produced. The Woolf Report[1] did not only look back. It also painted a broad landscape of how a prison service should be run. In its vision of security, good order, justice and links with the community the Woolf Report brought together many of the positive aspirations of the prison service.

Those of us who work in prisons always have to remember that we work on behalf of society. Prisons have no essential right to exist. They do so because society has decided that they should. For that reason, ordinary men and women have not only the right, they have the obligation to know what prisons are like and what goes on behind their high walls. Many people have a prejudice about what prisons should be like. Very few people have an informed opinion of what the options are. This book is a contribution to what is a necessary debate.

I have never been entirely at ease working in the prison system. If ever I were, it would be time to move on. That is more than a rationalization for what I do. One does well never to lose sight of the fact that prison is an abnormal institution. It may well be necessary to deprive some men and women of their liberty, but that does not make it normal. If prisons have to exist, then we should be quite clear what their purpose is, who should be sent to them and what they are meant to achieve.

Imprisonment is now a commonly used form of punishment in many countries across the world. The frequency with which it is imposed and the manner of its application differs from country to country. Western countries, and former colonial powers in particular, have left a terrible legacy in many countries where the use of imprisonment as a direct sanction is not indigenous. In the former totalitarian countries of eastern Europe prisoners had an economic function. Recent political changes have left prison administrations in these countries with a need for a complete reassessment of their practices.

The reservoir of wisdom about how society should deal with those of its members who breach its criminal laws does not lie exclusively in the developed world. Countries such as the United States, which now locks up a million and a quarter of its citizens at any one time, need to learn from the experience of other countries.

There is now a wide-ranging discussion about the need for alternatives to imprisonment. In due course we should begin to regard imprisonment as the alternative punishment, only to be used when there is no possibility of imposing a community sanction.

Where it remains necessary to deprive people of their liberty, this has to be done within the confines of a clearly defined set of national and international norms and guidelines. Many of these are already in existence. Those who work in prisons and in prison administration have to know what these norms are and be required to observe them. The public has to be aware that the prisons which are run on its behalf must be places where justice is the guiding star. This is not a soft option. Without it there can be no thought of prisons contributing to the prevention of future crime.

REFERENCE

1. Report of an Inquiry into Prison Disturbances April 1990 (1991), HMSO, London, Cmnd 1456.

TWO

The Beginning

THE GOVERNOR'S TALE

When I joined the prison service I had little understanding of the world I was entering. Prisons were, and largely still remain, outside the direct experience of most people. Twenty years ago they were little written or spoken of in the média. They rarely appeared on our television screens and were only referred to in the press when some particularly notorious criminal received a prison sentence.

On being admitted through the gates of Edinburgh Prison for the first time one had a superficial feeling of normality. The centre of the yard beyond the prison entrance was a well-stocked flower bed surrounded by a well-tended lawn. From the outside the buildings looked like many a hospital, school or army barracks. Built of red sandstone and brick, they were no more forbidding than many other institutions in which I had been.

This superficial normality continued when one saw groups of men in uniform walking about, to work, to the dining room, to the sports field, to chapel. One recognized that the person bringing up the rear and slightly to the side of any such group was wearing a different sort of uniform. On closer examination one noticed that he was the only one wearing a uniform cap and that he had a large set of keys hanging ostentatiously from a chain. Only he was able to open and close all doors through which the party passed.

The sense of normality disappeared at the beginning and end of each day. Every morning the men in blue uniforms unlocked the door of each cell on each gallery and men in grey or brown uniforms emerged, two or three from each cell. They were carrying plastic chamber pots full of urine or faeces which they deposited in the sluice sinks near the washbasins on each gallery. They then collected jugs of water from the basins to take back to their cells to wash and shave. At the end of each day the ritual was reversed. The men in grey or brown uniforms rushed to the toilet and to collect some water before being ushered into their cells by the men in blue uniforms, who then went around locking each door in turn.

If one had any doubts that this was an abnormal institution these were dispelled when one saw the sorry trail of visitors, usually women, who came to the wicket gate of the prison clutching passes to visit loved ones or friends. They were ushered into a small, dirty, smoke-filled room where they waited until their names were called. Then they were taken to an adjoining room where they found a row of cubicles with glass fronts and sides. The person whom they had come to visit was already sitting on the other side of the glass. The visitor took his or her place on the small bench which was fixed to the floor and spoke as best possible through the six inches of wire mesh which covered the space between the foot of the glass and the wooden ledge on which they leaned.

My first twelve weeks in the prison service were spent wearing one of these blue iniforms, opening cells, locking cells, escorting prisoners to visits, supervising them everywhere they went. I learned that it was necessary to change one's clothes immediately on returning home because the smell, which was the most recognizable feature of the prison, clung to one's work clothes and brought the reality of prison into one's home. I came to understand more about the nature of imprisonment during that twelve weeks than in any one period since.

In 1973 the training of assistant governors in the United Kingdom Prison Services was carried out in a 'sandwich course' which lasted for two years. This involved extended periods spent at the Prison Service Staff College in Wakefield, short spells with various other agencies such as mental hospitals, social work and probation departments and management training institutions. The bulk of the time was spent learning the technicalities of the job in a prison.

My initial reaction on going to the Prison Service Staff College was one of disorientation. There was little discussion about the purpose of imprisonment or the place of imprisonment in the criminal justice system. Instead we immediately entered a world of regimentation of the mind. Attention to detail was more important than understanding fundamental principles. The first requirement was to learn the fine print of 'standing orders' and 'circular instructions' and how they were to be applied. The basic reality of imprisonment was a given which was not open to question in any meaningful way.

So, from the outset I found myself in an environment which, from both a personal and a professional standpoint, was at the same time fascinating and frustrating. The human dynamics of being a member of a group of people who were responsible for depriving another group of people of their liberty presented a continual challenge. One had to question on a daily basis the manner in which this task was achieved. One had to cope regularly with the consequences for individual prisoners of rules and regulations which were drawn up primarily for the benefit of the institution of the prison.

It was inevitable that one was most conscious of the interface between the system and the individual prisoner during the first weeks and months of working in a prison. One had not become inured to the illogicality of many of the daily routines of the prison. One was not used to the concept that a rule should be obeyed simply because it exists, to the assumption that one individual is likely to be more or less trustworthy than another because of the type of uniform which he wears.

People who are not in positions of power or authority are often good judges of character or of another's state of mind. Children, for example, have a sixth sense which tells them which adults can be trusted and which cannot. In a similar way prisoners seemed to sense that a new assistant governor was someone likely to be open to influence. There were frequent calls to explain why a particular rule existed or why another regulation had to be applied in such a way. All of this served to heighten one's awareness of a need to indentify the features which are essential to the concept of imprisonment and to separate them from other elements which have been added on through practice over the years.

The frustration came when one tried to indentify these essential features of imprisonment from a study of internal sources. The statutory documents, such as the Prison Act and the Prison Rules, were equally unhelpful. All of them began from an acceptance of the inevitability of the existence of imprisonment. They said little about its purposes and less about when it was to be used.

In one of the letters which he was able to send to his wife while he was in prison, Vaclav Havel wrote:

> . . . I never feel sorry for myself, as one might expect, but only for the other prisoners and altogether, for the fact that prisons must exist and that they are as they are, and that mankind has not so far invented a better way of coming to terms with certain things. [1]

I knew that if I was to continue to work in the prison system I had to find out for myself why mankind had invented the prison and why it continued to be used so extensively when, by any obvious measure, it seemed to be so ineffective.

THE USE OF PUNISHMENT

The concept of imprisonment is inextricably linked with that of punishment, just as the concept of punishment is linked with that of order. All forms of society have found it convenient to impose some kind of order on their members. This is usually justified by the argument that the good of the majority must take precedence over the needs of individuals. The good of the majority may be stated in terms of some form of absolute, such as a moral code, or in situational terms. If this greater good is threatened by the actions of individuals, so the argument goes, they must be brought into line by some form of punishment.

Philosophers tell us that punishment of this kind has five main elements:

> 1. The person who undergoes it must experience suffering. There can be no punishment without pain or at least inconvenience. This presumes that punishment is personalized.

> 2. An offence must have been committed and guilt established. In other words, it has to be proved that wrong was done and that the person doing the wrong was responsible for what happened.

3. The punishment must be inflicted on an individual. That is to say, it cannot be inflicted on a group of people or on a corporate body. If several individuals are to be punished for the same offence, their personal responsibility has to be proved.

4. The punishment must be inflicted by a human agency. The natural consequences of a human action, such as the child burning her hand as a result of putting it in a fire, cannot be regarded as punishment.

5. Those who impose the punishment must have the legal authority to do so. Punishment, in other words, is different from vengeance. It must also be proportionate to the offence.

In Western society the state has increasingly taken on itself the duty of inflicting direct punishment on the offender. Crimes, even when committed against individuals, are generally regarded as offences against the state. This is in contrast to the situation which existed previously. Then the punishment of individuals invariably took account of the harm or damage done to the victim. Restoration and compensation paid by the offender to the victim, even for serious crimes such as murder, were important features of punishment.

There is increasing concern in Western countries that one consequence of what has now become the almost total involvement of the state in matters relating to the punishment of crime has been that the victim is now all but forgotten. This is most obvious in the manner in which criminal procedures have developed.

Let us suppose that a private citizen reports to the police that her house has been robbed. After she has given a statement to the police, her part in the procedure will probably be at an end. Unless the case is serious enough to attract public attention, she is unlikely to hear when and if an arrest is made. She will not be consulted by the prosecuting authorities and is unlikely to be told when the case is due to come to court. If she learns when the case is to come to court and she wishes to attend, she will have to make her way to the public gallery of the court so as to follow it. If the accused is found guilty, the victim will have no opportunity to indicate whether, in her view, she would be satisfied to receive an apology from the offender, or whether she would like him to offer some form of compensation. The victim may well feel as much violated by her exclusion from the process of the criminal law as by the offence itself.

This way of punishing offences is in sharp contrast to that which exists in what are generally described as developing countries. There it is quite common that the form of traditional law will provide for a senior member of the community to act on its behalf in reaching a settlement between the offender and the victim. This settlement will be based on a social equilibrium which takes account of reparation for the victim, the recognition of the offender's family responsibilities and the wish to avoid isolating offenders from their community. If property has been stolen or damaged, it will have to be replaced. If the breadwinner has been injured and is unable to support his family, the offender will have to provide for the family.

This traditional way of dealing with offenders was disrupted by the colonial legacy which foisted on many of these countries a legal process which was quite foreign to their culture. The legacy is a visible one. Many cities and towns in Central and South America, in Africa and Asia, have been left with prison buildings which architecturally are minor replicas of Wormwood Scrubs or its equivalent from another former colonial power. This inappropriate legacy is compounded by the fact that the economy of these countries makes the proper maintenance of this system of legal punishment impossible to support.

For very practical reason several countries in Africa are now actively exploring ways of finding modern expressions of these traditional forms of justice.[2] If they succeed in doing so, they will have an important lesson to pass on to the so-called developed countries.

Traditional forms of punishment in Western cultures were based in the community. They included reparation, compensation and fines. Execution was available for the most serious crimes. In many jurisdictions it was not commonly used.

The English tradition of extensive use of execution for crimes against property owed more to the need to maintain the existing balance of power between classes in society than to any strictly legal concept. During the twenty years at the end of the eighteenth century in London and the County of Middlesex 1,910 criminals were sentenced to death and 890 were executed. In Scotland, which had a population twice the size, during the same period 134 criminals were sentenced to death and only 97 of these were eventually executed.

Another method of punishment which was common in many traditional systems was the exile of the wrongdoer from the community, often for a set period. This was relatively easy in societies where movement from one area to another was comparatively rare. Chinua Achebe describes an example of how this practice operated in Nigerian society in his novel *Things Fall Apart*.[3] Okonkwo, a respected elder of his tribe, accidentally kills a man and accepts his punishment of seven years' exile to another tribe.

In British, and particularly English, criminal justice a more recent expression of this system of exile was the transportation of convicts to the colonies, first to the Americas and then to Australia. This linked the notion of exile to the very practical need to find abundant and cheap labour for these developing territories.

By the time the last convict ship sailed for Australia in 1867, an alternative form of exile from the community had been found: imprisonment. Until the eighteenth century imprisonment had been little used as a direct punishment by the court. It had instead been used mainly as a holding place, where prisoners were kept while they awaited trial, or for debts to be paid or for execution or exile.

THE GROWTH OF IMPRISONMENT

By the middle of the nineteenth century the principle of imprisonment as a direct punishment was becoming established in many Western countries. This was given an added boost in Great Britain with the abolition of transportation. At first the ships which had been used to transport the convicts to the colonies were moored in many of our major estuaries and the convicts used on public works, such as the great dockyards of the time. The conditions on these hulks were abominable and, as any seaman would have known, after they had been left to ride at anchor for a period they began to rot.

The solution was to build the great Victorian fortress prisons, many of which remain in use today. The conditions within them were much removed from those of the colonies and the transport ships. The principle on which they operated was entirely similar, that of exiling the prisoner from the community.

Organized religion must shoulder a great deal of responsibility for the development of the principles of imprisonment. Much of the barbarous treatment meted out to prisoners over the centuries has taken place in prisons which were nominally under the control of one or other Church. The form of imprisonment which remains common today in the Western world has its roots squarely in the Christian religion.

Students of ecclesiastical architecture and those of penal history might usefully contrast the hermitic cells of early monasticism, grouped around a central church building, with the Victorian prisons still in use today. These consist of tiers of rooms, also described as cells, grouped around what often remains the most impressive building in the establishment, the prison chapel.

The changes which were introduced in the way prisons were run in the last half of the eighteenth and first half of the nineteenth centuries confirmed that the similarities between the monastery and the prison went beyond that of architecture. Prisoners were to be separated from all negative influences They were to have no communication with each other. They were to be subject to 'good' influences such as the habit of regular work, frequent visits from the governor and the chaplain who, along with the medical officer, formed an all-powerful triumvirate to manage the prison.

Many of the individuals who led the way in reforming the management of prisons and the way prisoners were treated acted out of a clear sense of religious duty. Their activities were closely linked to the growing evangelical and Nonconformist traditions which viewed service to fellow humans as an expression of service to God. This was the personal perspective of the great English penal reformer of the late eighteenth century, John Howard:

> By his prison work he hoped to save the bodies and souls of prisoners, for he believed that only the grace of God had made him less depraved than they, and therefore able to minister to them.[4]

The new model prisons which were built in England, first in Sussex and later in Gloucester, were designed to take account of the prevailing philosophy of the time. Howard himself described this in the following terms:

> Solitude and silence are favourable to reflection; and may possibly lead them (prisoners) to repentance. [5]

The reformers, including Howard, who argued that prisoners should be separated from each other while in prison did so on grounds of reducing the negative effects of imprisonment. These were physical, in terms of hygiene and health, and moral, in terms of corruption and bad influence. The justification for separation was later extended on the grounds that prisoners could be subjected to good influence from indentified senior members of the prison staff, most notably the governor and the chaplain. From there it was a short step to advocating the possibility of personal reform which might spring from 'reflection'.

At the beginning of the nineteenth century much of the argument about how people detained in prison should be treated revolved around the 'separate' and the 'silent' systems. In the separate system prisoners were not allowed to mix with each other. They spent all day in their cells, being given a fixed quota of work to complete each day. In the silent system prisoners worked together but draconian steps were taken to ensure that they did not talk to each other.

In due course the separate system won favour over the silent system and became the basis for the future management of prisoners. It confirmed the aim of removing prisoners from bad influence and subjecting them to good.

It is usually held that this system had its roots in the Eastern Penitentiary in Pennsylvania, which owed much in its development to the influence of the Quakers. The separate system is sometimes described as the Philadelphia system.

In 1834 William Crawford, shortly to be appointed government Inspector of Prisons for the Home District of England, was sent to America to observe this system of imprisonment. He reported that:

> The Eastern Penitentiary is, in fact, with some trifling difference in its arrangements, but a counterpart of the Bridewell at Glasgow, a prison which was in operation

five years before the erection of the prison at Philadelphia.[6]

This form of prison discipline had been developed in Glasgow Prison by the governor, William Brebner, a remarkable man who had a great influence on the development of the prison system in Scotland.

The first government Inspector of Prisons for Scotland, Frederic Hill, described in detail how the system in Glasgow Prison operated:

> At six in the morning throughout the whole year, the prisoner begins his daily work, and, with short intervals, continues to labour till eight in the evening, when his hammock is brought into the room and he goes to bed; and this round continues day after day and night after night. Through the whole period of his confinement, he scarcely ever sees the face or hears the voice of a fellow prisoner; and this total seclusion from the corrupting society of his companions is brought about without the infliction of great mental suffering or severe pain of any kind, as is proved by the fact (of which there is little doubt) that the prisoners enjoy as high, nay a higher degree of health while in the Bridewell than persons of the same class of life do when at large. And instead of being a heavy burden on society, . . . the prisoners in the Glasgow Bridewell earn by their labour nearly the whole of their maintenance, including the salaries of those officers whose superintendence they have rendered necessary by their own acts.
>
> The nature of the employment is very various, extending from the single process of picking oakum to the somewhat difficult art of print-cutting; so as at the same time to suit, as far as possible, the different powers of the prisoners and the demand for labour in the surrounding district.
>
> The work allotted to the prisoners is calculated to employ them about 11 hours a day; that is , about the same time as is occupied in most of the factories in the country.[7]

The efforts of early prison reformers were concentrated more on the way prisons were run rather than on what they were for. Then as now the reformers faced a dilemma. The more the state of prisons was improved, the more courts seemed prepared to use them. New prisons were built to replace old ones. What often happened was that the new ones became additions to the old ones rather than replacements. Wandsworth Prison was built in 1850 to replace the run-down Brixton Prison. When the newly built Belmarsh Prison opened in South London in 1991 Brixton was, and still remains, in use and little changed.

All of this bore out the dictum of Alexander Paterson, a Prison Commissioner for England and Wales between the wars:

> Wherever prisons are built, courts will make use of them.

During the years of extensive prison building in England in the second half of the nineteenth century the greatest users were the lower courts. In 1857 the number of people sent to prison by the higher courts was 12,189. In 1877 this had fallen to 9,793. For the same period, in contrast, those sentenced to imprisonment by summary procedure rose from 86,795 to 144,562.

JUSTIFYING THE USE OF IMPRISONMENT

Although the first efforts at reform had concentrated on how prisons are run rather than on what they are for, it was not long before new arguments were produced to justify the increased use of imprisonment as a direct punishment of the court. Its use as a punishment which consists of the deprivation of liberty was not regarded as sufficient. Other forms of justification had to be provided. These gradually focused on some imprecise notion of the reform or rehabilitation of the person who was in prison. This principle was summarized in the report of the Gladstone Committee on Prisons in 1895 which boldly affirmed:

> . . . we start from the principle that prison treatment should have as its primary and concurrent objects, deterrence and reformation. [8]

Leaving aside the inconsistency in suggesting that there could ever be more than one primary aim, this statement overlooked the fact that the primary object of imprisonment is to deprive people of their liberty.

It was no coincidence that this rationalization gained credibility at a time when work in prisons was becoming more respectable. The growing need to justify the use of imprisonment as a punishment in its own right coincided with the introduction of 'experts' into the prison system: chaplains, teachers, instructors, psychologists, psychiatrists and social workers. Jailers sought respectability and became known as governors; warders became known as prison officers.

The wish of those who worked in prisons to present a more positive face to their daily task was understandable. Suppose someone asks me what my job as a prison governor involves. I may reply, 'I lock people up.' I don't feel too good about that response and probably the questioner will feel less than positive towards me. If, on the other hand, I reply, 'I reform people and rehabilitate them', I can feel good about that and the questioner is likely to warm towards me.

The Scandinavian criminologist Nils Christie recognized this sentiment:

> (It) makes life somewhat easier for the personnel within these institutions. The hangman's job was never very popular. Those who got a chance slipped into the doctor's role as fast as possible. There are great amounts of ambivalence in having direct responsibility for other people's suffering. There is a need for a defence. Major strategies are to claim that what one is doing to other people does not hurt, is intended to help, or actually is very efficient in helping them even though it might hurt a bit in the beginning – just like so many good cures. [9]

The tentacles of this argument reached into every part of the prison system. The new professions of psychology and psychiatry welcomed the opportunity to extend their work to a captive group of subjects. They assessed, measured and predicted every aspect of a prisoner's behaviour. This 'medical model' of imprisonment was a secular expression of the religious perspective of individual guilt, expiation and punishment. In this new world, the prisoner was seen as someone who had to be cured of his criminality, who had to be made well again. Release was to be determined not solely on the basis of a punishment served but also on the basis of individual response to 'treatment'. Even the description of imprisonment was changed. Prisons became institutions, prisoners became inmates. In some countries the prison system became known as the department of correction, guards became known as correctional officers.

The first prison reformers had started out with the simple aim of improving prison conditions for their own sake, of making prisons places which were clean, well-ordered and where prisoners were treated decently. Where this later went wrong was that the humane and decent treatment of people in prison was linked to some vague principle of what became known as reform or rehabilitation.

> The merit of Sir Alexander Paterson's campaign in the 1930s – and that of Sir Lionel Fox and other penal reformers later – was to emphasize, in addition to the *right* of the State to punish, the *obligation* of the State to provide facilities for education and treatment on grounds of humanity and social justice. The shortcoming of their aims – and the weakness that lies at the centre of the present debate – is that they coupled the ideas of education and treatment of prisoners with that of crime prevention, in the belief that this would be an important way of reducing individual recidivism.[10]

The parameters of the debate about what prisons are for were set largely by those who worked within the system. They were set in an age which had an inherent belief in the power of one group of people to change the behaviour of others. During its golden age after the First World War the confidence of its proponents was unbounded. Alexander Paterson expressed this succinctly:

> The problem of recidivism is small, diminishing, and not incapable of solution.[11]

The notion that prison could be used as a means of forcing a cure on the people who were held there led to changes in both the sentencing process and the length of time people were held in prison. It led to courts passing sentences of indeterminate length. Only in exceptional cases does a 'life' sentence mean that the offender will spend the rest of his or her life in prison. It means that a decision on release will be made outside court according to some imprecise opinion about when the person has been 'cured' of his or her criminality.

The same principle led to semi-determinate sentences, such as that of borstal training. This sentence had a minimum and a maximum length. The actual time spent in prison was not decided by a court but by prison administrators on the basis of assessment about how well the young man or woman had responded to the experience of imprisonment. This principle also, in theory, underlies the practice of releasing prisoners before the end of their sentence under community supervision. This system is usually known as parole.

One can understand why people who work in or about prisons should be keen to promote the notion that sending people to prison might help to deter others from committing crime or could lead to those who had been in prison being more likely to keep the law once they had been released. People may reluctantly accept that resources should be channelled towards prisons on the grounds that such resources will assist in rehabilitation and, therefore, may eventually help to reduce the future crime rate. They are not likely to agree to the need for additional resources for prisons on the basis that, while they will not contribute to crime prevention, they should be available for prisoners out of respect to him or her as a person. This will be particularly true in an age when all public expenditure is coming under greater scrutiny.

The suggestion that people should be sent to prison to deter either themselves or others from committing crime, or as a way of reforming their behaviour, in other words as a form of crime prevention, may have provided some professional respectability for those who work with prisoners. In the short term, it may have been useful as a means of convincing the purse holders of the need to expand the prison system. The proposition certainly carried within itself the seeds of its own failure.

Despite the expansion of the prison system it became clear that the rate of crime in society was being little affected. The rate at which prisoners committed further offences after release bore little relation to the length of time they had spent in prison. This led to the criticism that prisons were not fulfilling their objectives. Questions were asked about how they used the resources which they were given. The credibility of the system was called into doubt.

This would not have been an issue had it been accepted that the only justification for sending people to prison is as a means of depriving them of their liberty, either because the safety of the public demands it or because of the serious nature of the crime which they have committed. The future life style of a person who has just been released from prison will not depend primarily on how he or she has been treated in prison. It will depend on whether he or she has decent accommodation in which to live, has a job or some other source of income which will provide a decent standard of living, has family or friends who will provide care and support.

The relevance of imprisonment rates to general crime rates can be shown by reference to some of the statistics from Western countries. The rate of imprisonment is usually shown on the basis of the number of prisoners for every 100,000 people in the country. In September 1990 the figure for the United Kingdom was just over 90, in France it was 82, in West Germany it was 78, in Denmark it was 63, in Italy it was almost 57, in the Netherlands it was 45. In the United States of America the figure in 1992 was a staggering 455, by far the highest proportion of any country for which we have reliable figures. In real terms this translates into a million and a quarter people in prison in the United States. There might be a practical justification for this rate of imprisonment if one could say that as a consequence the United States was the safest place in the world to live. That is not the case.

The story so far applies primarily to Western countries, and those which follow their tradition, such as Australia and New Zealand. In totalitarian countries the situation has been somewhat different. By and large such countries have been reluctant to recognize the existence of crime. The alternative has been to hold that large groups of people should not be recognized as full members of society. These have included all those who are regarded as 'different' for whatever reason, usually because they do not accept the prevailing political ideology.

The usual way of dealing with such people has been to exile them from society, just as in Western countries. The nature of the exile has, however, been quite different. In many countries an alternative society has been created. Its members have no rights of their own and are required to work for the benefit of the general economy. Its members have usually been required to live, not in Western-style prisons but in large labour camps. The work done in these camps has until recently been an integral part of the economy of the country.

The nature of this alternative society has been vividly described by Zhang Xianliang, who spent 22 years in Chinese labour camps and who recounted his experiences in *Getting Used to Dying*.[12] In a factual manner, for example, he described how prisoners had to fill bags with the bones of deceased fellow prisoners, it did not matter which bones. When relatives came to collect the remains of their loved ones the camp authorities simply stuck the required name on the already waiting bag.

The complex system of labour camps, known as the gulag, which was set up in the former Soviet Union is another example of this phenomenon. Valery Abramkin, a scientist sentenced to 6 years in prison in 1979 for human rights activities and now Director of the Public Centre for the Promotion of the Humanization of the Soviet Penitentiary system, has described the system in the following way:

> The Gulag is not a penal system, but a huge complex which uses manual labour to produce income for the state. The criteria for release are dictated by targets for industrial production: the good worker stayed inside, the difficult prisoner, often with a far worse criminal record, was freed. Officials at the Interior Ministry agree that this has played a part in the soaring crime rate.[13]

Speaking at a recent seminar on prison reform,[14] General Yuri Kalinin, head of the Russian Prison Service, described the reality of the recent past. The operation of the penal system was linked directly to the national economy. Prisoners were transferred thousands of kilometres, without any thought being given to their personal circumstances, to meet a shortage of labour in a particular region. Up to 200,000 prisoners could expect to be moved in this way during any one year.

The foundations of these prison systems have now collapsed with the changed economy. Full employment in society, however contrived, has now given way to soaring unemployment. There is very little work available for those in the labour camps. Their means of subsistence, always precarious, have all but disappeared.

The situation has been described in similar terms by an eminent Hungarian criminologist:

> After the Second World War there had been a strong belief that socialist regimes would also offer social justice. Criminals were perceived as the political enemies of the system. Crime was committed against society. The emphasis was on removing offenders from society. This resulted in very high prison populations. The centralized economy meant that all prisoners worked and received a wage. Industry benefited from employing prisoners because wages were lower. Many factories provided hostel accommodation with full board for ex-prisoner employees. The situation has now changed. Rising unemployment is likely to affect offenders more than any other section of the community. There is no tradition of providing aftercare. The few probation officers have low social status. Support for the families of offenders is minimal. Public opinion towards offenders is hardening.[15]

END THOUGHTS

At a fairly early stage in my voyage of inquiry into the roots of prison systems, I had made two important discoveries. The first was that the use of imprisonment had expanded in a very ad hoc manner which had little to do with developing concepts of justice. The second was that most of the justifications for the use of imprisonment were based on as erroneous belief in what it might achieve. In Western countries these were centred on a belief in the reforming influence of the prison. In other traditions they were related to the provision of cheap labour.

The truth is that the *act* of putting people in prison, depriving them of their liberty, is essentially negative. It should only happen on one of two counts, when the safety of the public requires it or when the offence which has been committed is so serious that no other punishment would be acceptable.

Once a person has passed through the gates of the prison, it is the responsibility of everyone who is subsequently involved to ensure that the *experience* of imprisonment is as constructive and as positive as is possible. Let us move on to find out whether this is what happens.

REFERENCES

1. Havel, V. (1990), *Letters to Olga,* Faber & Faber, London, p.270.
2. These and similar subjects were extensively discussed at a seminar on penal reform in Africa which was held in Banjul, the Gambia, in July 1992.
3. Achebe, C. (1958), *Things Fall Apart,* Heinemann, London.
4. Condon, R. H. quoted in McConville, S. (1981), *A History of English Prison Administration,* Routledge & Kegan Paul, London.
5. Howard, J. (1972), *The State of the Prisons in England & Wales,* reprinted (1973) by Patterson Smith, New Jersey.
6. Quoted in the Annual Report of the General Board of Directors of Prisons in Scotland for 1840, HMSO, London.
7. Report of the Inspector of Prisons for Scotland (1836), HMSO, London.
8. Report of the Departmental Committee on Prisons (1895), HMSO, London.
9. Christie, N. (1978), 'Prisons in Society, or Society as a Prison', in Freeman, J. (ed.) *Prisons, Past and Future,* Heinemann, London.
10. McClintock, F. H. (1983), 'The Dilemma of Penal Reform Today', in *Journal of the Association of Scottish Prison Governors,* vol. 2, 1983.
11. Ruck, S. K. (ed.) (1951), *Paterson on Prisons,* Muller, London.
12. Zhang Xianliang (1991), *Getting Used to Dying,* HarperCollins, London.
13. *Financial Times,* 6 November 1991.
14. A Training Forum organized by the Council of Europe for Directors of Prisons in Central and Eastern Europe, held in Warsaw, Poland, 5–9 October 1992.
15. Professor Katalin Gonczol of Budapest University speaking on 27 September 1990 at a seminar organized by Penal Reform International in Budapest.

THREE

The Reality of Prison

THE GOVERNOR'S TALE

During the last few years the public in the United Kingdom has become much more aware of prisons than was ever the case before. There have been two main reasons for this. The first is that many people who work within prison administration have realized that there is nothing to be gained from maintaining the prison as one of the last great secretive institutions in our society. The result of adopting that stance until recently was that the public and the media assumed that the prison system had something to hide. The press made full use of any snippet of information which came their way. Invariably this was about an incident or dramatic occurrence which was then reported from a critical point of view.

The change of attitude on the part of prison administrators has not been entirely self-motivated. In 1981 two independent Inspectors of Prisons were appointed in the United Kingdom. The Chief Inspector of Prisons deals with prisons in England and Wales and in Northern Ireland. The Chief Inspector of Prisons for Scotland deals with that country's prisons. Both Chief Inspectors publish the reports of their inspections of individual prisons as well as an annual report of their activities. The Chief Inspector for England and Wales has been particularly open in his criticism and this has obliged the Home Secretary to respond publicly.

The second reason that the public has become more aware in recent years of what goes on in prisons has been the succession of major incidents which has occurred in prisons across the world. It is very difficult to be secretive when prisoners are on the roof of a prison in full view of television cameras, when they burn a prison to the ground or when they break out at gunpoint.

Despite this relative openness most members of the public still know almost nothing of what passes for 'normal' in daily life inside a prison. This is hardly as it should be since prisons are run on behalf of society. Everything which is done inside them is done in the name of society. Society and its members have not only a right but an obligation to know what goes on behind the high prison walls.

Informed members of the public may know comparatively little today about what goes on in prison. Twenty years ago, they knew even less. When I joined the prison service I prided myself on being reasonably well informed about national and international affairs. About what life was like for a prisoner or a prison officer, I was singularly uninformed.

Like many large prisons in Scotland at the time, Edinburgh Prison contained several different kinds of prison inside its perimeter. It was the newest prison in the country, having been built largely by the labour of prisoners in the 1920s. The layout inside the prison walls was quite generous. The accommodation blocks, known in Scotland as halls, stood separate from each other, joined to one another by a covered corridor. A well-proportioned chapel stood in the middle of the prison. Dotted around the prison were well-tended areas of grass and flower beds. A series of well-equipped workshops stood at one end of the prison. At the other end a new kitchen and a set of dining halls had just been built. Beyond them was a sports field.

FIRST IMPRESSIONS

All of this went unnoticed by the prisoner on first admission. He had usually appeared at court that morning and had been remanded in custody. If this was his first court appearance, he had probably been remanded 'for further enquiry' for seven days, what was known among prisoners as 'a seven-day lie-in'. He was brought to prison under police escort and taken to the reception area. His personal belongings were handed over to the prison staff by the police and the court warrant was checked. This was the legal justification for depriving a person of his liberty and had to be exact to the last detail. The prisoner was then shown into a small cubicle to wait until prison staff were ready to process him.

In describing this procedure, one is struck that all the verbs used are in the passive form. That is no accident. From the moment he entered the prison, the prisoner became to all intents and purposes a passive player to whom things were done. The last thing expected of him was any form of active response.

The small cubicle in which the prisoner had to wait was quite claustrophobic. The sole piece of furniture was a small strip of wood fixed to the wall in a way which allowed the prisoner to sit rather uncomfortably. While doing so he would be able to extend his arms to either side so that his elbows touched the walls. He would be able to touch the door in front of him without moving. He would be only too well aware that the door had no handle on the inside and that it was bolted on the outside. He had no choice but to sit quietly until he was called for.

Edinburgh Prison received prisoners from a number of courts, some of them quite a distance away. One problem was that police tended to deliver prisoners within a fairly short scale of time each day, following the end of court business. This meant that all the administrative work for those prisoners being received each day had to be done in a very short space of time. There was little opportunity for taking account of the personal stress or trauma which a person who was faced with the first complete loss of liberty was likely to be going through.

The only members of staff in reception were those prison officers who were responsible for seeing to the logistical side of the work: checking warrants, taking fingerprints and photographs, checking personal property, filling in the numerous forms and files which the prison bureaucracy demanded. A prison nurse officer visited reception to make a cursory inspection of newly admitted prisoners. After a few superficial questions, the officer shone a lamp on the prisoner's private parts to discover whether there was any obvious infection. The prisoner could then expect to be seen by the medical officer the following morning.

Losing one's liberty is one of the most traumatic experiences any individual is likely ever to undergo. There was little recognition of that in the way people were treated when they came into prison. As soon as possible individuals were given a number. Their clothes and personal possessions were taken from them. They were required to bathe. They were issued with a uniform. From that moment the private person ceased to exist. He was replaced by an anonymous figure with a number and a surname.

This dehumanizing process made it easier for staff to carry out their tasks in a neutral way. Their first priority was to ensure that the system ran smoothly. Prisoners were received into prison, their identity was checked, they were allocated to a cell. There was no opportunity to sit down with a prisoner, to explain to him the reality of the new world which he had entered, to listen to his fears and expectations, to discuss how the loose ends which he had inevitably left undone would be attended to, to consider the effect which his imprisonment would have on family or people who depended on him in one way of another. All these matters might well be attended to in succeeding days, but at the point of admission, at the point of greatest stress to the person who had just been imprisoned, the needs of the system came before the needs of the individual.

THE UNCONVICTED PRISONER

Once the reception process had been completed, the prisoner would be taken to the accommodation block which would be his home for the period of his imprisonment. Unconvicted prisoners were held separately from those who had been convicted. The principle on which this separation was based was the legitimate one that the person who had not been convicted and who was therefore innocent, should not be required to mix with those who were criminals. The practical consequence of the separation was that conditions for unconvicted prisoners were much more restrictive than those in which the convicted were held.

The resources available to most prison systems are limited. When it comes to allocating these resoures unconvicted prisoners have fared badly. There is a general assumption that they will only be in prison for a relatively short period. In Scotland all criminal trials must begin no later than 110 days after the prisoner has been taken into custody. Such prisoners are also regarded as in many ways the responsibility of the prosecutor.

Unconvicted prisoners cannot be obliged to work, although prison rules stipulate that they should be offered the opportunity to do so. As a consequence most unconvicted prisoners in Scotland in the early 1970s spent 23 hours each day in their cells, allowed out only to go to the toilet and to collect water at infrequent intervals, to collect their meals and to take one hour's exercise.

Most prison cells have enough space to hold only a single bed, a small desk, a chair and perhaps a small cupboard. The floor space left between the bed and the table is only wide enough for one person to walk up and down, taking about three paces before having to turn. In most cells there would be a small window placed high up in the external wall, which allowed in a limited amount of natural light and provided very little vision. Prisoners in Edinburgh were relatively fortunate in that the windows were full-length and gave some outlook, even if it was only on to a high wall.

One of the guiding principles of imprisonment in the Western world has been that prisoners should spend a considerable amount of time on their own, contemplating the error of their ways and considering how they might improve their behaviour after release. For that reason prison cells were built to accommodate one person. Having a room of one's own, even one with no handle on the inside of the door, is a luxury which few unconvicted prisoners in Great Britain enjoy. Two and sometimes three people are crammed into a small room which was built to hold one person. The only change to the furniture of the cell is the replacement of the single bed by two bunk beds.

Most of us would find it difficult to spend the majority of each day for weeks on end confined in a room with one person, even one whom we loved dearly. Unconvicted prisoners are often required to live literally cheek by jowl with people whom they do not know and with whom they have nothing in common other than the fact that they are all prisoners.

That in itself would be bad enough. But there was one feature which made overcrowding of this nature in Edinburgh Prison, and most similar prisons, even more abominable. Despite the fact that they were confined to their cells for such long periods each day, prisoners did not have constant access to toilet or sanitary facilities. They were able to go to the toilet at the beginning and end of each day and often at meal times. For the rest of the day they were dependent on the good will or availability of prison officers to allow them out when they pushed the alarm button in their cell. At all other times they were obliged to make use of a small chamber pot.

This was a demeaning and humiliating experience. The best part of twelve hours would pass between the time prisoners were locked up at night and were allowed out the following morning. It was hardly less demeaning but none the less understandable that many prisoners would resort to defecating into newspapers which they then threw out of the cell window. A small group of prisoners, known as 'the bomb squad', had the task of going round the prison each morning to clear up the detritus. One of the most abiding sensations for anyone, prisoner or member of staff, in a prison where these insanitary practices prevailed was the revulsion of the early morning procession of rows of men taking overflowing chamber pots to the toilets on each landing. These pots were emptied into sluices which stood close by wash-hand basins where men did their best to maintain some form of cleanliness.

The main feature of the regime for unconvicted prisoners was its sheer blinding monotony. The dark green and dirty cream walls oozed apathy. The overpowering sensation was one of deadening regimentation. The only thing which the 150 prisoners in the accommodation block had in common was that they were all awaiting trial. Some were undergoing their first experience of imprisonment, quite out of their depth in the new world into which they had been thrust. Others were regular visitors, petty criminals for whom a spell in prison was an occupational hazard. A number were facing serious charges of murder, violence or robbery. Young men between the ages of sixteen and twenty-one years were kept in the same hall but were not allowed to mix with the older prisoners.

Imprisonment did not affect only the man who was in prison. It also completely changed the way of life of his immediate family. In most cases the main source of income for the family was cut off. If the prisoner had been in employment, his wife and children would be left dependent on state support. For those unused to a criminal way of life, the family would suffer social stigma and might well be ostracized.

According to Prison Rules, unconvicted prisoners were entitled to receive one visit each day, lasting for fifteen minutes. The visit room consisted of rows of small glass-enclosed cubicles. Two visitors squeezed into one side of the cubicle, separated from the prisoner whom they had come to visit by a pane of security glass. Conversation was carried out through a small grille at the bottom of the glass. The fifteen-minute period was hardly long enough to begin a conversation about any of the pressing issues which might well be outstanding. Instead, it would be filled with a discussion of trivialities. For the prisoner it also meant a precious fifteen minutes out of his cell. For the wife who visited each day, there might well be the prospect of a long, tedious and expensive journey by public transport to and from the prison, often with one or more small children in tow.

SHORT-TERM CONVICTED PRISONERS

Convicted prisoners in Scotland were divided into those serving long sentences and those serving short sentences. A short sentence was eighteen months or less. Prisoners in this category served their sentence in the prison closest to the court in which they were sentenced. For most of them this meant staying relatively close to home. All such prisoners in Edinburgh Prison were held in one accommodation block. The population here was a transient one. Many prisoners would be serving sentences of a month or less. Some of them would be in prison for failure to pay a fine and would be released within a matter of days. All prisoners serving over five days were entitled to remission of one third of sentence for good behaviour. This meant that a person sentenced to, say, thirty days' imprisonment would be released after twenty days.

The hall in Edinburgh Prison which held the short-term prisoners had the atmosphere of a disorganized poor-house. There was a sense of continual movement, of comings and goings. Prisoners were invariably held two to a cell. Activity began shortly after staff came on duty at six o'clock in the morning. Once staff had peered through the small glass spyhole in each door to check that every prisoner was accounted for, the malodorous procession to the ablution area began.

This was always a period when tension, like the contents of the chamber pot, could spill over. Fifty prisoners, some still half asleep, others with pent-up frustration after a sleepless night during which they had been wrestling with thoughts of the life which they had left behind, jostled for access to one slop sink, half a dozen wash-hand basins and three toilets. A wrong word could lead to an angry response. Violence was never far below the surface. It was also a favourite time for more calculated violence, for settling old scores brought into prison from life on the streets, for wreaking vengeance on someone who had been convicted of what was considered to be an unacceptable crime. It would be a matter of moments for one or other prisoner to distract the attention of the prison officer supervising the activity. There would be a quick, unidentifiable flurry. Then a prisoner would be left lying in the corner with blood streaming from a smashed face. Another case of 'slipping on some soap in the shower, sir'.

By quarter past seven prisoners were making their way in procession to the dining room for breakfast. The inevitable porridge was accompanied by a piece of bacon or a sausage, by bread and a pint of tea. Prisoners went straight from breakfast to work. A number went back to the hall to begin cleaning and general household tasks. The majority went to one or other of the large workshops. Sewing mailbags was still the order of the day for many. They would sit in ordered rows with swathes of pre-cut hemp which had to be made up into bags, an exact number of stitches to the inch. Other prisoners would go to the mat shop where they hammered large coir doormats into shape, mats which would eventually be sent to other prisons and to most government offices in Scotland. The air in this shop was always thick with dust. Other prisoners worked in a shop where they broke down old telephone cables and separated the parts which could be salvaged for future use.

The activity in the different shops varied greatly, depending on the interest shown by the instructor, on the aptitude of the workers and on the rates which they were paid. There was usually a fair degree of activity in the coir shop, where the instructor was always on the move, discouraging inactivity. The coir had to be banged and battered into shape with brushes and hammers. This was a popular way of venting many of the frustrations of being in prison.

The mailbag shop was known as the 'pool' party. It accommodated prisoners who had not yet been allocated to a work party as well as those who had been found to be unsuitable for other work. To go into that workshop was to enter another world, even within the context of the prison. When one walked through the door one understood what was meant by the description of prisons as the dustbins of society. Regimented in rows were broken men, with sallow faces and sunken eyes, clinging to their humanity; those who could not cope; those to whom society had given the label of failure. For them prison was the ultimate asylum, the last place of safety.

For a few moments each morning workshops took it in turn to become hives of activity. This was when the governor made his magisterial tour, accompanied by the chief officer. In through one door, given the number of prisoners in the party by the officer who acted as doorkeeper, a brief word with the instructor and out by the second door. It was all over in a moment and torpor could be restored.

By eleven thirty all tools were handed in and accounted for. Prisoners processed back to the dining hall for lunch, which was the main meal of the day. After lunch they were all shepherded into the broad pathway outside the hall where the next hour was spent walking aimlessly up and down, taking the statutory 'exercise' in the fresh air. If it was raining the alternative was to return to the hall where prisoners made their way onto the four galleries and walked round and round the landing for an hour.

After that it was back to the workshop until tea time. Occasionally the monotony might be broken by a visit to the doctor, the prison welfare officer or a visiting social worker. From time to time the chaplain might visit the workshop and the opportunity could be taken to engage him in conversation for a spell despite the obvious irritation of the instructor.

At quarter past four tools were handed in and checked by the instructor against the shadow board which hung from the wall in his office. Prisoners lined up at the exit door and were subjected to a perfunctory rub-down search by the officer who was in charge of security. All of this was to ensure that no tools were taken back to the accommodation halls, where they might be fashioned into weapons.

After tea prisoners were locked in their cells, alone with their cell mate and their thoughts. On one evening a week they might have the chance of coming out for a few hours to watch television or to play snooker or table tennis. On another evening during the winter months there might be a meeting of Alcoholics Anonymous or a hobby class. At 8.30 p.m. prisoners were given a pint of tea and a bun. They also had a last opportunity for a visit to the toilet and to collect some drinking water.

The highlight of any evening would be if a prisoner had a visit from family or friends. Three visits were allowed every two months. Each lasted for thirty minutes and took place in the same cramped surroundings used during the day by prisoners who were on remand.

The time allowed hardly permitted the beginning of any real discussion or the maintenance of any genuine family contact. Prisoners would look forward to the visit with high expectation. All too quickly it was over and they returned to their cell in a very subdued frame of mind. The route back to the hall passed the line of sight of the gatehouse and prisoners would delay the procession, hoping to gain a last glimpse of their visitors passing out of the prison.

By 9 o'clock staff had taken a final check of numbers and were going off duty. A quiet descended on the hall and a stranger would find it hard to believe that 200 men were lodged behind the various cell doors. From time to time a recently admitted prisoner would be suffering from the symptoms of alcohol withdrawal or would be highly mentally disturbed. Then the silence would be broken by an irregular cacophony. Sometimes a prisoner would constantly bang a chair or even the heel of his shoe against the heating pipe which ran along one wall of his cell. This would set up an echoing resonance which could be heard throughout the hall and in each cell. At other times the prisoner would repeatedly batter a mug or other utensil against his cell door in a way which no one could ignore. If this went on for more than a few minutes there would be a response from other prisoners. At first a few catcalls and cries for silence. If it went on for any length of time there would be a protesting outcry from other prisoners which would build up into a deafening crescendo of noise until staff quietened the first prisoner down or took him out of the hall.

The pointlessness of many prison sentences and their wastefulness in human terms were immediately obvious in the part of Edinburgh Prison where short-term prisoners served their sentences. Few of these men presented any danger to the public, few required the punishment of deprivation of liberty. By and large they were the casualties of our materialistic society, unable to survive the pressures of modern living; petty offenders, who persistently committed minor offences.

As a type, they were personified by Billy, a fifty-year-old man who looked more like seventy. The longest sentence which he had ever served was nine months. Cumulatively, he had served the equivalent of a life sentence. His job in prison was to sweep the main corridor which connected the accommodation blocks. The day before he was due to be released he would seek out the Chief Officer and remind him to keep his job vacant for him until he returned. And he invariably did.

LONG-TERM CONVICTED PRISONERS

In the early 1970s a long-term prisoner in Scotland was defined as someone who was serving over 18 months. For those serving these longer sentences there were three options. Men who had never been in prison before were held in a separate section of Edinburgh Prison. Those who had been in prison before, but who were thought to be 'trainable' were sent to Perth Prison. Like Edinburgh, Perth was a generic prison which also held unconvicted and short-term convicted men from its own catchment area. Those who were considered to be 'untrainable' were sent to Peterhead Prison, which will be described in a later chapter.

If a man responded well to the regime at Peterhead Prison he could expect in due course to be sent to Perth Prison. Similarly, once in Perth Prison he would eventually be considered for a transfer to Edinburgh Prison. From Edinburgh he would move, shortly before release, to an open prison or to a 'Training for Freedom' hostel.

There were almost 200 prisoners in the two halls of Edinburgh Prison which made up the training wing. Those who had never been in prison before were referred to as first offenders. In reality, many of them had a long history of encounters with the criminal justice process. It was more by luck than good judgement that they had never before received a prison sentence.

A number of prisoners were genuine first offenders. Among this group were many of those serving life sentences for murder. The reality now, as then, is that one is more likely to be murdered by someone whom one knows than by a complete stranger. Most of them had committed their crime when under the influence of alcohol. They might have gone out for a drink on a Friday or Saturday evening. The next thing they remembered was waking up the following morning in a police cell to be told that they had killed someone. They had become involved in a drunken brawl. Not infrequently it was a matter of chance as to who was the murderer and who was the victim. Generally these men were model prisoners. Many of them found it difficult to come to terms with the fact that they had taken another human life. Their inner anguish, which at times became black despair, was more of a penalty than any prison sentence.

The daily routine of the long-term prisoners was largely similar to that of the short-termers. Most of them had a cell to themselves. There was slightly less regimentation in their routine. They had a wider variety of workshops, which included printing and bookbinding, light engineering and woodworking. Some of them were given training in painting and decorating or joinery. There was an opportunity for part-time education, ranging from remedial work to certificate courses and Open University. On most weekday evenings there was 'association' between 6.30 and 8.30. This might include recreation such as watching television and playing indoor games or evening classes.

Men who came into the long-term category were allowed to have one visit each month. These visits took place on a Saturday or Sunday afternoon in one of the dining halls. Unlike the area where the unconvicted and short-term prisoners had visits, this room was large and airy, rather like the works canteen which one would find in any major factory. The prisoner and his visitors would sit around the table. A prisoner would come round with a trolley of tea and biscuits which the visitor could purchase since prisoners did not carry cash. The prisoner was allowed to hold hands across the table with his wife or girlfriend. A quick embrace was allowed at the beginning and end of the visit. If children came they were expected to sit quietly at the table.

The monthly visit was the emotional climax in the monthly cycle of existence for many prisoners. During the days before it took place a man would think of little else. Other prisoners would know that he was on edge and would leave him plenty of defensive space. Experienced officers would recognize this too and step back a bit. Occasionally an officer who had taken a dislike to a particular prisoner would deliberately push him at a wrong moment in order to get a reaction which might end up with an appearance before the governor on a disciplinary charge. If things went badly at the hearing the visit might be cancelled. More likely, the governor could order that it should be a 'closed' visit which would take place in the room used by short-term prisoners.

On the morning of the visit the prisoner would arrange to have a shower, to take particular care with his toilet. After the midday meal he would put on a freshly ironed drill shirt and change into his Sunday best grey uniform. The hour or so before the visit would drag interminably while he rehearsed in his mind everything which he wanted to say to his visitor, who would usually be a wife or a girlfriend. For many of the younger prisoners though, the visitors would be a mother and father.

At a superficial level the visit would go well. Everyone would be polite to each other, would discuss the weather and what the traffic had been like on the journey to the prison. The prisoner would assure his visitors that everything was going well. The visitors would tell the man interesting snippets about neighbours or how well children were doing at school. And then the shouted command from the officer in charge would tell everyone that the hour had passed. People had to move quickly to allow the second group of visits to take place.

The prisoner would go back to his cell with a sense of despair at all the things which had been left unsaid and which could not be said for another month, if even then. It was impossible and unwise to expose any real feelings in such a public place and over such a short period of time. Through his own emotional aridity he would be aware of all the matters which had been left untouched. How his wife had not mentioned the difficulty she must be having in making ends meet, the pressure of dealing with children who responded badly to comments made in the playground about the fact that their father was in prison. Prison did not allow, did not encourage, men to recognize or to admit to these pressures publicly. They had to be dealt with in the secrecy of one's own cell.

The task of management in respect of men serving short sentences was primarily to ensure that they completed their time in prison with the minimum of fuss. For those serving long sentences the task was more complex. They were the subject of regular reports which recorded their behaviour in prison. On the basis of these reports decisions were made about when a man should be 'upgraded' to less secure conditions, either within the prison in which he was serving his sentence or in another prison.

The most important reports written on a prisoner were those prepared when he was being considered for early release on parole. For those serving determinate sentences this came when one third of the sentence passed by the court had been served. The process started for those serving life sentences after they had completed seven years in prison. The earliest such a man could hope to be released was after nine years in prison. It was the need for all these reports to be written which had led to the introduction of the new grade of assistant governor in the late 1960s.

For many men the knowledge that these reports were being written about them was a form of exquisite torture. They had little or no opportunity to contribute to them. Very often they would not know when they were being written. Given an option they would have opted out of the process. Yet they knew that any progress through the system, to a better job, to another prison and ultimately to release, depended on what went into these reports. It was like jumping through a set of hoops while blindfolded.

The most traumatic experience came with consideration for early release on parole. For a man serving a sentence of any length the difference between release at one third of sentence and at two thirds of sentence meant a substantial difference to the time spent in prison. The process began some five months before the due date when the prisoner was asked if he wished to be considered for parole. If he did, the long bureaucratic process began. Reports on the prisoner were written by prison officers, by welfare officers, by the chaplain, by the education officer, by the workshop instructor. A social worker would visit his family home to confirm that it was a 'suitable' address for him to be released to. Finally the prisoner would be interviewed by an assistant governor who then compiled all the other reports into a comprehensive dossier. The prisoner saw none of these reports. His only direct contribution was the opportunity he had to write a personal letter to the Parole Board giving reasons why he felt he would benefit from parole.

There would then be a wait of several months while the reports made their way through the administrative machinery. Eventually, a matter of days before the prisoner's parole date, a decision would come. It was brief and to the point. Addressed to the governor of the prison, it either instructed that the prisoner should be released under supervision or that the Secretary of State had decided that he should not be released and that his case would be further considered the following year.

It was the task of the assistant governor to pass the decision to the prisoner. If the decision was positive a period of hectic activity followed, making final arrangements and alerting supervising officers. If, as was more often the case, the decision was against early release the assistant governor would try to work out with the prisoner why this conclusion had been reached. It might be because of the nature of the crime, it might be that officials thought that the due penalty had not been exacted, it might be that they were of the opinion that there was a risk of reoffending, it might be that the man had not responded in the way expected of him in prison.

For most men serving long sentences the year was divided into two parts. The first half was spent preparing the case for parole and waiting expectantly for an answer. The second part was spent recovering from the disappointment of a refusal and wondering whether it was worth going through the process again the following year. Some decided that it was not and opted out of the process, preferring the certainty of release after two thirds of the sentence had been served. Most persevered, hoping against the odds that this time they would be successful.

In many respects the parole system epitomized the way in which the long-term prisoner was managed. There was a crude but effective balance of carrot and stick. Prisoners knew that the date of their release could be determined by the way they behaved in prison. The more courses they applied for, the more positive reports were likely to be. The more they learned to speak to the right people, the better impression they would create. The system did not look for a profound change of attitude; it looked for proof of ability to respond in an acceptable way to the discipline of the prison.

INHUMAN AND DEGRADING TREATMENT

In all but a few minor details that picture of a large local prison as it was twenty years ago could have been painted yesterday. There may be a fresh coat of paint on the walls. In some cases buildings will have been rebuilt. But the reality for the prisoner remains substantially as it was. In many respects things have become worse.

The number of people in prison has increased substantially. Until recently this was not matched by any significant increase in the amount of accommodation available. In 1973 the average number of people in prison establishments in England and Wales on any one day was 36,774. By 1983 the figure had risen to 43,462. During financial year 1991–1992 the daily average population had risen to 47,746. This latter figure included an average of 1,310 people held in police cells. In each of the same three years the Prison Department reported that there were respectively 35,391, 38,806 and 45,527 available spaces. [1]

These statistics hide the reality that overcrowding in prisons in the United Kingdom is concentrated in local prisons. It is understand-able that the prisons which hold those serving long sentences should be protected from overcrowding. The price paid for this arrangement is that those prisoners who are awaiting trial, that is, those who are yet to be found guilty of any offence, and those who have received short sentences, that is, who have been guilty of less serious offences, are held in the most overcrowded conditions.

Many local prisons are over 100 years old and occupy cramped inner-city sites with few facilities. In his annual report for 1990–1991 HM Chief Inspector of Prisons commented on what this meant:

> It is to be regretted that for many prisoners, and particularly those on remand, their first custodial experience is of a cramped, claustrophobic, and poorly equipped establishment. [2]

The spartan nature of local prisons extends beyond the state of the buildings. The basic standards of health and hygiene in many prisons have changed little since Victorian days and are not acceptable at the end of the twentieth century. The daily process of 'slopping out' human waste still continues. The government has given a commitment that by the end of 1994 every prisoner in England and Wales will have access to sanitation at all times. We can take little pride that it has taken us so long to provide such a basic entitlement. Facilities are now being provided with such speed in order to meet the given deadline that one wonders at the long-term wisdom of what is being done. Our professional successors are likely to express surprise that in many instances we saw fit to install toilets in living accommodation; an arrangement which some prisoners view as providing a toilet in a bedroom, while others choose to see it as having a bed in a lavatory.

In most local prisons the facilities which are provided to keep prisoners occupied are minimal. For a variety of reasons they have decreased over the last twenty years. The majority of prisoners can measure the hours out of cell each day in single figures. Boredom is still the prime feature in the lives of many prisoners.

In July and August 1990 members of the European Committee for the Prevention of Torture and Inhuman or Degrading Treatment or Punishment visited several prisons in England. The committee visited three major local prisons for men: Brixton, Leeds and Wandsworth. It reached a damning conclusion:

> . . . the cumulative effect of overcrowding, lack of integral sanitation and inadequate regimes amounts to inhuman

and degrading treatment. This is a matter that needs to be addressed with the utmost urgency.[3]

AN INTERNATIONAL PROBLEM

The practice of holding those prisoners who have not yet been found guilty of any crime in particularly restrictive conditions is not peculiar to the United Kingdom. It happens throughout the world in countries where general standards in prisons are extremely spartan.

Butyrka Prison is one of the main remand prisons in Moscow. It was built in 1871 and was originally used as a starting-off point for those who were to be exiled to Siberia. It is on a cramped inner-city site, hidden behind high buildings. It was designed to hold 3,500 prisoners. In November 1992 it held 5,200 prisoners, of whom 452 were women. There were 580 staff. 4,500 of the prisoners were awaiting trial. There are few restrictions on the public prosecutor in Russia in respect of the time which he can take to investigate the case against any accused. It is not uncommon for a prisoner to wait several years to come to trial. During this period the public prosecutor decides to which of the limited facilities the accused may have access. It frequently happens, for example, that the prosecutor will instruct the director of the prison that a prisoner who is awaiting trial may have no visits from his or her family. Such prisoners may have visits from a lawyer, if one is retained in the case, but no special facilities are available for consultations. Lawyers will frequently have to queue outside the prison to learn first if their client is in that particular prison and then to wait for a visiting space.

Overcrowding is a major problem. The main prison is made up of 25 large accommodation blocks. Prisoners are held in large rooms, each with anything between 25 and 50 beds. In late 1992 in one large room, which the authorities said had space for 40 people, there were 90 prisoners. In that room there were 70 beds. The unlucky ones without a bed of their own slept in shifts. There was a toilet in a screened-off area in one corner. Personal washing was draped on lines of string. Most rooms had electric sockets and in a few prisoners had supplied a television. They spent the whole day in these cells, with little to keep them occupied.

Little has been done to renovate the prison and it is now in a very poor condition of repair. The authorities have few resources to improve conditions. In the present state of the economy paint is very hard to come by, let alone materials for structural improvements.

A Western journalist who visited Kresty, the main remand prison in St Petersburg, which has if anything a worse reputation than the Butyrka, painted a similar picture:

> When a warder unlocked one of the cells, so many miserable faces peered out from the gloom it was hard to count them. At last I got an accurate tally: nine men squeezed inside a space just 15 ft long by 9 ft wide. The cell was filthy, and the stench of men living like animals in a cage was overpowering. Some crowded on to the two three-tier wooden bunk beds that were pushed against the walls. The others had been issued with bedding, a skimpy mattress and a thin pillow, but there was no room to unroll them, no space to lie down to sleep. One prisoner said he slept with his head resting over the cell's toilet, a hole in the ground.[4]

The Central Prison in Banjul, the Gambia, is thousands of miles away from Butyrka and Kresty but in relative terms life for remand prisoners in July 1992 was remarkably similar. They were held twelve to a room. A number of them slept on planks stretched between two concrete plinths. The remainder slept on the ground in spaces between and underneath the planks. These sleeping conditions were quite claustrophobic. Prisoners were not issued with mattresses for fear that they might set them alight. The prisoners were allowed to circulate in a small adjoining compound for several hours in the morning and again in the afternoon.

The Nigerian Civil Liberties Organization undertook a three-year project of monitoring prison conditions in the country and has published its findings.[5] The general picture is a frightening one. Prison overcrowding is so severe that many prisoners have to take it in turns to sleep. One group will stand around the walls of the cell while the remainder sleep on the floor in cramped and totally unhygienic conditions. Prisoners depend to a large extent on their families for food, clothing and medication. Almost 60 per cent of those in prison are awaiting trial. Their conditions are often the worst of all. Periods of up to 10 years awaiting trial are not uncommon. The Nigerian Institute for Advanced Legal Studies found that 3.3 per cent of those on remand had been in custody for over 15 years.

Similar tales could be told of how people who are awaiting trial are treated in many prison systems across the world. In several countries the fact of arrest leads to a presumption of guilt. The principle of being innocent until proved guilty has a very hollow ring about it in practical terms.

END THOUGHTS

Many of the most depressing aspects of the prison systems in the United Kingdom are demonstrated in the large local prisons which hold prisoners who are awaiting trial or who have been sentenced to short terms of imprisonment. A typical local prison will be between 100 and 150 years old. Physical conditions, for staff and for prisoners, will be spartan. The fabric of the buildings may generally be in a poor state of repair.

More often than not there will be severe overcrowding. A survey carried out among prisoners in England and Wales in 1991 [6] indicated that 82 per cent of remand prisoners had to share a cell with one or more people. 71 per cent of convicted prisoners in local prisons had to share. In local prisons the major part of each 24 hours is likely to be spent in these cells. Among the convicted prisoners in these establishments 34 per cent said they were locked up for more than 20 hours each day. Among remand prisoners, the figure rose to 58 per cent. Meals are usually eaten in cells.

There will be restricted private access to sanitary facilities. Opportunities for showering will be limited. Changes of clothing will be rationed.

Deprivation of liberty places severe strain on family and other relationships. Visits in many local prisons are severely restricted in respect of length and frequency. The conditions in which visits take place often make any sort of meaningful discussion of shared problems very difficult.

In some respects one can describe any prison system as the conscience of society. Within the walls of the prison the veneer of politeness which covers most human relationships is stripped away to be replaced by a naked clarity which goes right to the heart of how each of us feels about our fellow human beings. The social pressures of courtesy and good manners are stripped to a minimum. Sometimes there is a reverse pressure if a man or woman has been found guilty of or even charged with a crime which we find repugnant or which has attracted a great deal of public outcry.

The large local prisons which hold the majority of prisoners on remand or those who have been convicted of minor offences are not glamorous places. In many respects they are places of hopelessness and failure.

The justification for treating men and women who are in prison decently is that they are fellow human beings. Whether they are treated decently and with respect is a major test of the civilization of any society and a challenge to those who administer a prison system. Our treatment of prisoners, of those we have labelled as outcasts, is a mirror image of our own human dignity.

REFERENCES

1. Reports on the Work of the Prison Department for 1973 and 1983; Report on the Work of the Prison Service April 1991–March 1992, HMSO, London.
2. Report of HM Chief Inspector of Prisons, January 1990–March 1991, HMSO, London.
3. Report to the United Kingdom Government on the visit to the United Kingdom carried out by the European Committee for the Prevention of Torture and Inhuman or Degrading Treatment or Punishment (1991), Council of Europe, Strasbourg.
4. Jack Chisholm, *The Sunday Times*, 10.6.90.
5. 'Behind the Wall, A Report on Prison Conditions in Nigeria and the Nigerian Prison System' (1991), Nigerian Civil Liberties Organization, Lagos.
6. Office of Population Censuses and Surveys (1992), The National Prison Survey 1991, HMSO, London.

FOUR

Women Prisoners

THE GOVERNOR'S TALE

Prisoners are usually referred to in the masculine gender. This is not entirely sexist. Women make up between two and five per cent of virtually every prison population across the world. It was not always so. When the General Prison at Perth in Scotland was opened in 1842 one in three prisoners was a woman. For several reasons special consideration needs to be given to women who are deprived of their liberty.

I have never worked in a prison for women but I have come across them twice in my career. There is one women's prison in Scotland, at Cornton Vale near Stirling. In the early 1970s the one women's prison was at Greenock in the west of Scotland. In several other male local prisons there was a small unit for women who were on remand. There was one such unit in Edinburgh Prison. It never held more than half a dozen prisoners. The staff were all women. A few of them were permanent officers who regarded Greenock Prison as their main station and served for a few years in this female outpost. The remainder of staff had temporary appointments, several of them being the wives of officers in the male prison.

The management of this small unit came under the main prison. The assistant governor had to go in on a daily basis to listen to any requests which the women had, to prepare reports for court appearances and to deal with disciplinary matters. One was immediately struck by the personality of the six or seven women who were held in this insular little unit. The atmosphere was less that of a prison and more that of a nineteenth-century asylum. Staff were guards certainly but maternal in a disciplined manner. The women, dressed in shapeless smocks, had an appearance of inadequacy and dependence. From time to time one of them would be highly disturbed and quite violent. Occasionally male staff from the main prison would have to come into the unit to help to subdue any woman who was particularly volatile. Underlying the gleaming floors and dust-free window sills was an air of drabness and despair.

I had no direct responsibility for any women prisoners for another twenty years until I became governor of Brixton Prison. The main prison for women remanded in custody from any court in the south of England is Holloway in north London. The level of security at that prison means that it is not suitable to hold a woman who is in the highest security category. A separate area within the high security unit at Brixton Prison has been converted to hold such prisoners. It is rarely used but from time to time a woman may be remanded in custody, perhaps charged with a terrorist offence, who has to be held there.

Since the outstanding charges are likely to be serious, it may be that the woman has to remain in that unit for many months in virtually solitary confinement. Clearly there must be no contact with the other prisoners, who are all male. Exercise in the fresh air is difficult since the yard is overlooked by other prisoners. The unit has a day area, a kitchenette and a washing area as well as three cells. The woman is allowed free movement within this area during the day hours and often builds up a friendly relationship with the staff who have to take care of her. Unless she receives visits from family or friends the staff of the prison will be her only human contact.

These two limited experiences of working with women prisoners have brought me into immediate contact with the main features which set women in prison apart from their male counterparts.

FEWER WOMEN MEANS FEWER PRISONS

Since the proportion of women in the total prison population is so small there is generally little flexibility in providing accommodation for women prisoners. In most countries women are kept in dedicated prisons, although in some instances they are held in separate wings within male prisons.

In England and Wales there are few prisons for women. These are subdivided into establishments for young prisoners, for those on remand, for those convicted women who require close security and for those who require minimal supervision. This means, for example, that a woman who is remanded in prison from any court in the southwest of the country will be sent to a prison near Bristol; a woman from anywhere in the south of the country who is suitable for conditions of minimal security will go to a prison in Kent, and a young woman who needs to be kept under close supervision will go either to Essex, to West Yorkshire or to Cheshire.

In countries such as Canada, the United States and Russia women prisoners may be sent to prisons thousands of kilometres away from their home area. In many other countries there is only one prison for women.

The main outcome of all of this is that it is likely to be even more difficult for women who are in prison than for men to maintain contact with family and friends. The consequences for a family of a wife or mother being sent to prison are likely to be quite traumatic. If a father or husband is imprisoned the wife will generally make every effort to keep the family together. She will be quite skilled at making ends meet, at caring for the children, at simply surviving, even to the extent of travelling long distances regularly with small children to see her imprisoned partner. If the mother is sent to prison the reality may be quite different. For a start, the children, particularly if they are young, may well be taken into care. The father will be less likely to be able to care for them on his own and to bring them to visit their mother in prison. Even if this is possible, young children will find it even more disturbing to spend only a few hours a month in a formal setting with their mother.

In many prisons attempts are made to have such visits in a setting which allows less formal contact between mother and children. Several prisons in England have made arrangements for children to be with their imprisoned mothers regularly for a full day and to make use of prison facilities such as the gymnasium and education unit. [1,2]

Another consequence of the limited accommodation is that

women prisoners frequently do not have access to the same level of facilities for education and training as men. In Canada a woman who receives a sentence of more than two years is required to begin her period of imprisonment in the federal prison for women at Kingston in Ontario, regardless of where her home is or where she was convicted. The alternative is to stay in a provincial prison for short-term prisoners, where facilities are likely to be much more restricted. There are federal prisons for men serving a similar length of sentence in various parts of the country. Some years ago a woman who was being held in Kingston obtained a transfer to a prison for men in British Columbia so that she could be closer to her husband who was seriously ill. Some time later the federal government entered into a compulsory exchange agreement with the provincial government of British Columbia and attempted to transfer the woman to a provincial prison for women. In 1991 she obtained a court judgement that such a transfer would cause her 'irreparable harm' because she would not have access to educational facilities in the provincial prison and she was being transferred solely because she was a woman.[3]

It is not a simple matter to find a solution to the problem of dispersed accommodation for women prisoners. The Woolf Report suggests a resolution within the context of its recommendation that large local prisons should be subdivided into separate, autonomous units capable of holding remand prisoners, young offenders and, provided security is up to standard, women prisoners.

> It must be preferable to have women in a wholly secure and separate block under their own governor and staff and with full access to families within a local prison near to their home rather than, as at present, to have to hold them many miles from their homes and families.[4]

Some practitioners hold strong views on the subject of keeping women within predominantly male prisons even if total segregation can be guaranteed. At a practical level it is argued that given the proportionate numbers women will be marginalized and will not have full access to the various facilities which are available. If resources have to be allocated, the men will always have more than their fair share.

Other commentators point out that many women who are in

prison have been subjected throughout their lives to physical and sexual abuse by men. Ironically for some of them prison provides a place of safety where they can be sure that they will not be subject to abuse. To place them in close proximity to male prisoners will inevitably place unnecessary and inappropriate psychological pressure on them which will outweigh any benefit to be gained from such an arrangement.

THE WOMAN PRISONER AS MOTHER

There is now an increasing understanding that the prisoner is not the only person to be affected by the fact of imprisonment. Members of the immediate family and other relatives suffer as the result of the imprisonment of a loved one; none more so than those for whom the prisoner is a mother.

Only where there is a real threat to public safety should an expectant mother be held in prison. If this is necessary she should be given all appropriate antenatal care. It is hard to envisage any circumstance in which it should be necessary for a mother to give birth in prison rather than in a civilian hospital.

Arrangements vary from country to country for the care of babies whose mothers are in prison. In many jurisdictions prisoners are allowed to keep their babies with them while they are nursing, for anything between nine months and three years. If this does happen, it is preferable that the baby should be with the mother at all times rather than merely for an hour or so each day, as happens in some countries. Babies who are not in the constant care of their mothers should be looked after by qualified staff. Health visitors and other community paediatric services should be available in prisons.

There is debate about the age at which young children should be taken away from mothers who are in prison. Research carried out in England in 1988[5] found that the cognitive and motor development of young children who spent four months or more with their mothers in prison was retarded. When reaching a decision about whether a young child should stay with his or her mother in prison, much will depend on what the alternatives are. The situation of a young child who is to be taken care of by a grandmother, an aunt or some other close relative is likely to be different from that of a baby who is to be taken into local authority care.

REMAND PRISONERS

The proportion of women prisoners who are on remand, about 22 per cent, does not differ greatly from the equivalent statistic for men. What is different is that a significantly higher proportion of such women do not subsequently receive a custodial sentence. Less than a quarter of women who are remanded in custody subsequently receive a custodial sentence. The fact that a high proportion of all those remanded are not subsequently sentenced to imprisonment can be attributed to several factors such as criteria for refusal of bail. It may also be that the sentencing court takes into account the length of time a person has spent on remand. But none of these factors account for the differences between the outcome for men and for women. There is no evidence that women who are charged with offences are more likely to commit further offences, to abscond or to threaten witnesses than are men. If anything, the contrary might be thought to be the case.

Proportionately more women than male prisoners have been convicted of non-violent offences such as theft, handling stolen goods, fraud or drug offences. There is no obvious reason why a higher proportion of women should be remanded in custody rather than on bail. There are proportionately fewer bail hostel places for women and this may be a factor. Research carried out with remand prisoners at Holloway Prison in London[6] goes as far as to suggest that refusal of bail may sometimes be used as a punishment.

> The majority of women on remand eventually receives a non-custodial sentence. If the alleged offence is such that this outcome is likely, there seems to be no persuasive argument for remand in custody.

MENTALLY DISTURBED WOMEN

Recent research carried out at Cambridge University[7] concludes that in many cases women are remanded in custody, not because their actions or offences are dangerous, but because the courts think that they need psychiatric help. This partly reflects the reality that many of these women do in fact need some form of help. . However, the Cambridge research showed that remand in custody was a very inefficient manner of seeking psychiatric help. As with men in a similar situation, women remanded for psychiatric reports are held in prison longer than those on simple remand.

> A custodial remand is not only an inhuman and inefficient method of obtaining inpatient care for mentally ill defendants. It is also an ineffectual method of obtaining non-residential treatment for those mentally ill offenders – the majority – who require treatment but not hospitalization.

The research found that many of these women could have more appropriately been dealt with under existing procedures for diversion from the criminal justice process to a health or social service provision.

A survey of 708 women who were admitted to Holloway Prison in 1986 found that 195 of them had a previous record of self-harm, 125 had a history of psychiatric illness, 99 were dependent on opiates and 89 regularly took psychotropic drugs. It concluded that less than half were free of any evidence of psychological disorder. [8] This finding was confirmed by research carried out on behalf of the Home Office in 1991 which found that 56 per cent of all women held in prison in England and Wales had mental health problems. [9]

A report by the National Association for the Care and Resettlement of Offenders [10] points out that because women prisoners tend not to embark on riots or other mass disturbances one should not assume that they do not have difficulties with being in prison. On the contrary, women will often show their distress by turning their violence on themselves. There is a consistently high level of self-mutilation in women's prisons. According to published statistics, it would appear that discipline is more rigorously enforced in women's prisons. A frequent comment from women who have served prison sentences is that discipline is imposed in a petty manner. [11,12]

END THOUGHTS

I have come across some terrible prisons in the last twenty or so years in many countries, including the United Kingdom. The one which shocked me most of all was a women's prison in Romania. There was no immediate evidence of physical brutality although one was inevitably concerned at the fact that, as in many countries, several of the staff who were directly responsible for the women were men. There were two features of the prison which had a considerable effect on me. The first was that the women were dressed in smocks with brown and white vertical stripes which were so evocative of concentration camps. The second was the shower area. It included a large ante room with bench seating around the walls where the women removed all clothing before going into the shower room. This was a large, bare room. Protruding from the ceiling at evenly spaced intervals were forty shower heads. There were no cubicles, there was no privacy. One could picture the women being herded in, naked, for their weekly shower. The whole area reeked of the humiliation which these women must have gone through each week.

Locking up human beings, depriving them of their liberty is a grave punishment. It is particularly traumatic when applied to women. The consequences of deprivation of liberty, the removal of so many fundamental aspects of human integrity, of individuality and of personal responsibility have a particular resonance when the person being so treated is a woman.

The ultimate justifications for imprisoning women are the same as for men. There are some women in every society who have committed such terrible crimes, who are such a threat to the public, that they must be deprived of their liberty. The personal, domestic and societal consequences for a woman of being locked up in prison are such that a court must be doubly careful before sending her there. The evidence from many countries across the world is that women are sent to prison not because they are a threat to the rest of us but because they are perceived to have broken some of the stereotypes which men have of women as mothers and as wives, and therefore because they are thought to be 'mad rather than bad'.

This is a sad reflection on a male-dominated criminal justice system.

REFERENCES

1. Report on the Work of the Prison Service, 1990–1992, HMSO, London, Cmnd 1724.
2. Report on the Work of the Prison Service, 1991–1992, HMSO, London, Cmnd 2087.

3. Referred to in Penal Reform International (1993), Introduction to Human Rights Training for Commonwealth Prison Officials, PRI, London.
4. Report of an Inquiry into Prison Disturbances April 1990 (1991), HMSO, London, Cmnd 1456.
5. Catan, L (1988), The Children of Women Prisoners: What are the Issues? in Morris A & Wilkinson C (eds), Cropwood Conference Series, No 19, Institute of Criminology, Cambridge.
6. Casale, S (1989), *Women Inside*, The Civil Liberties Trust, London.
7. Grounds, A et al (1991), Mentally Disordered Remand Prisoners, Home Office, London.
8. Turner and Tofler (1986), Indicators of Psychiatric Disorder among Women Admitted to Prison, *British Medical Journal*, vol 292, 1986.
9. Gunn, J et al (1991), Mentally Disordered Prisoners, Home Office, London.
10. National Association for the Care and Resettlement of Offenders (1991), A Fresh Start for Women Prisoners, NACRO, London.
11. Peckham, A (1985), *A Woman in Custody*, Fontana, London.
12. Carlen, P (1983), *Women's Imprisonment*, Routledge and Kegan Paul, London.

FIVE

Young Offenders

PLAYING THE GAME

The prison service is one of the last institutions in British society which does not recognize individuals as adults until they have reached the age of twenty-one. Young people may be married, may have children, may even be divorced; they may have fought for their country in any corner of the world; but, in the eyes of the prison service, if they are not yet twenty-one they are not to be considered as adults. The basis of this distinction is largely historical.

When concerned individuals began to take an interest in prison conditions towards the end of the eighteenth and throughout the nineteenth centuries one of the first areas of criticism was the lack of any separation among groups of prisoners. Untried and convicted, men and women, young and old were herded together in squalid and unsupervised conditions. One of the first tasks which the reformers set themselves was to make sure that different categories of prisoner were held separately from each other, in the hope that the influence which older prisoners had on the young, which the mature had on the immature, would be kept to a minimum.

In 1835 a Select Committee of the House of Lords recommended that there should be a separate penitentiary for juveniles. Three years later a former military hospital at Parkhurst on the Isle of Wight was converted into a prison to hold boys between the ages of ten and eighteen years. If a regime which included armed guards, leg irons, whipping and solitary confinement represented an advance on previous arrangements, one shudders to think what it must have been like before. The boys' prison at Parkhurst closed in 1864.

The Youthful Offenders Act of 1854 allowed voluntary agencies to set up reformatory schools under the supervision of the Home Office as an alternative form of custody for juveniles. The Children's Act of 1908 abolished imprisonment for juveniles under the age of fourteen and also placed restrictions on the imprisonment of those between the ages of fourteen and sixteen.

The Gladstone Report of 1895[1] suggested that the years between sixteen and twenty-three were crucial in the maturation of habitual criminals. The Gladstone Committee was aware of the regime at Elmira Reformatory in New York, which was based on the principle that young people should be reformed rather than punished, and it was an experiment along these lines which the report recommended. In 1908 the Prevention of Crime Act provided for a separate regime for young men between the ages of sixteen and twenty-one. They were to be held in borstal institutions where the regime was to be based on a system of progression and rewards for positive response. The sentence was a semi-determinate one, lasting between one and three years.

Between 1922 and 1946 the English Prison Commissioner who had particular responsibility for the borstal system was Sir Alexander Paterson. He organized borstal institutions as pale reflections of the public school system. Staff were taken out of uniform. Education was given a high priority. House masters and matrons were appointed. Paterson summed up his philosophy in the following words:

> Borstal training is based on the double assumption that there is individual good in each, and among nearly all an innate corporate spirit which will respond to the appeal made to the British of every sort to play the game, to follow the flag, to stand by the old ship.[2]

The Scottish Prison Commissioners had at first resisted the notion of separate institutions and regimes for young offenders based on an age criterion alone. They argued that greater flexibility was necessary and that prisoners should be separated according to individual need. But they were subsequently carried along on the tide of public enthusiasm and in 1911 they purchased Blairlodge School, 'a large private boarding school for gentlemen's sons situated at Polmont, Stirlingshire'. In December of that year it was opened as Scotland's first borstal institution. The enabling statute had authorized the Secretary for Scotland to come up with a suitable name to replace 'Borstal', so called because of the location of the first such institution near Rochester in Kent, but the Scottish Secretary never got round to doing so.

The world of borstal was to be my next experience after Edinburgh Prison.

THE GOVERNOR'S TALE

One morning in early December 1975 I received a letter from the Establishment Officer at prison service headquarters in Edinburgh. It was brief and to the point:

> Dear Coyle
> It has been decided to transfer you to be Assistant Governor II at HM Institution Polmont and I am writing officially to ask you to make arrangements for the removal of your furniture etc to Polmont where quarters are available.

Personnel management was not a highly developed skill in the Scottish Office in the mid 1970s. I resisted the temptation to respond with an inquiry as to whether the 'etc' included my wife and children. The obligation to occupy a prison quarter involved selling our own house in Edinburgh and moving into tied accommodation. These circumstances, allied to the fact that there had been no prior consultation about the move, did not leave me in a particularly positive frame of mind about taking up my new appointment.

Despite these reservations, there was an anticipation in going to work with younger men. Among the older prisoners at Edinburgh there had never been more than a fleeting prospect of being able to influence their future behaviour. The environment of the prison was generally one of dulled acceptance. There was little expectation that anyone would be changed for the better by the experience of imprisonment. The best one might hope for was to make the daily reality a bit more tolerable.

Within the borstal system, on the other hand, there was still a sense of optimism, that young men who were given proper training and support might mature and grow into law-abiding citizens. This optimism was most obvious among the small coterie of staff who had spent most of their professional lives in the borstal system and who had a sense of vocation about their work.

The physical difference between a prison for adults and a borstal institution became obvious when one approached Polmont Institution, as I did one morning early in 1976. Much of the campus of the former 'school for gentlemen's sons' remained untouched. Despite the fact that Polmont was the main secure borstal institution in Scotland there was no perimeter fence. A low stone wall separated the generous grounds from the main road. The sweeping tree-lined drive passed between a large vegetable garden and two football pitches. These fell away in a grassy terrace onto a well-tended cricket square which faced what had been the main house of the school. By 1976 this had been converted into office space.

The main accommodation units were known as houses. In prisons each wing was managed by an assistant governor. In borstal these same people were known as housemasters. There was a usual complement of staff: principal officers, senior officers and officers. In contrast to the prison setting these staff wore civilian clothes. In addition each wing had a matron. She would previously have been an officer in the women's prison and had the rank of principal officer. In common with her counterparts in boarding schools across the country, she had little power but a great deal of influence.

The original houses in Polmont had been given the names of Scottish historical figures: Douglas, Bruce, Wallace and Carrick. Douglas House held those who had most recently arrived while they were 'assessed'. Those who were thought to be in need of close supervision, who were in some way inadequate or who were likely to be put under pressure by others, were placed in Bruce House. The young men who were allocated to Wallace House were generally seen as strong characters, well able to look after themselves. Carrick House was a small, modern 24-place unit which held young men who were disturbed or unstable.

By the mid-1970s the pure philosophy of the borstal system was becoming diluted. The housemasters had reverted to the more usual title of assistant governors. Two new accommodation blocks had been built at Polmont in the early 1970s. They were known prosaically as East and West Wings. Following on from this, Wallace House became known as North Wing. A separate block, which had previously been a remand unit, became South Wing and Douglas House became the Allocation Centre.

My first appointment at Polmont was as assistant governor in the Allocation Centre. Officially the young men in borstal were known as trainees. Within Polmont they were known universally as 'lads' regardless of the fact that many of the older ones were married and some had children. At the start of his sentence every trainee spent six weeks in the Allocation Centre. The discipline there was particularly strict. John Steele, who passed through Polmont in the early 1970s, has described his first experience in the Allocation Centre:[3]

> We were taken to the Allocation Centre, where everyone spends a few months when they first enter Borstal. As soon as we entered I could see guys in immaculate gaol uniforms marching here and there in military fashion, the warders screaming, 'Left, right! Left, right!' We were pounced upon immediately by warders, who yelled at us to march. We didn't have a clue – at least I didn't – and I was slapped about the head for being out of step. When I turned to see who was hitting me I was slapped and punched from behind by another warder who shouted at me to face the front and keep my shoulders back. All the humiliation and brutality were deliberate: nothing was ever done to change the system because those responsible believe it works.

Steele goes on to paint a picture of a regime which swung between brutality and petty restriction; of being allowed no more than two minutes in the toilet; of having to say thank you to matron when collecting meals from the hot plate, whether she was there or not; of having to fold up one's bedding exactly to the last inch; of regular beatings by staff for any failure to reach the required standard. That was not the borstal of the official literature. Was it the borstal which I knew?

The answer to that question lies in the murky world between the official and unofficial. There was still a genuinely held body of opinion that the formation of the young male was best achieved by taking him away from his own environment and placing him in 'a man's world' where he would be moulded by being subjected to regular discipline and the positive experiences of a strict routine which included physical activity, education and training. This philosophy was not peculiar to the criminal justice process. Rather, its use there was an attempt to mirror the examples which were to be found in many other walks of British public life, notably the boarding school and the armed forces. There were many strengths to such an argument, but there were also many weaknesses.

In the first place, the environment was artificial. Young men were isolated from the influences which, for good or bad, had affected them in their formative years. The implication was that they should forget these, should respond to a completely different set of influences for one or two years and should then return to their original environment as changed people.

The abnormality of this environment was compounded by locking up some four hundred young people in early manhood in a single-sex society. The worst excesses of an exclusively male culture inevitably came to the fore. Success was measured by physical achievement. Sensitivity was interpreted as weakness. The extreme attitudes of the Scottish male were allowed to flourish unchecked.

In such an environment it was no surprise that the edge between discipline and brutality became blurred. This applied to the way the young men responded to each other and to the way staff dealt with them. The rules did not allow for any form of corporal punishment. It was known, however, that in one particular wing if a young man broke any of the rules in a minor way he would be given the option by the principal officer of having the charge dealt with formally by the governor or being given speedy physical punishment. Arguably that was little different to the experience which many of us had in boarding school. That principal officer was generally regarded as one of the better members of staff.

There was a deliberate policy of enforcing a martinet form of discipline in the Allocation Centre, which was the first experience which young men had of the institution. They were drilled and paraded daily. They were expected to move everywhere at the double. They had to stand to attention when they were being addressed by members of staff. They did not speak unless they were spoken to.

It was common that newly arrived assistant governors were first appointed to the Allocation Centre. This was a period of acclimatization for them just as it was for the borstal trainees. Experienced staff would test out the extent to which the new governor would allow them to have a free hand in enforcing discipline and how closely unofficial discipline would have to reflect the official rules.

My test came quite early. Each morning trainees who were accused of minor breaches of discipline were brought before the wing governor to have their cases dealt with. The principal officer was always present in the office during the proceedings. While dealing with one such case the trainee began to protest his innocence quite aggressively, although not in a way which I felt was out of order. Without warning the principal officer, who was standing slightly behind the young man, delivered him an almighty blow to the back of his head and told him that he should not speak to the governor in that manner. I was more taken aback than the trainee but quickly realized that how I responded would determine how the wing was to be run during my stay.

I continued as if nothing had happened. I asked the trainee if he had anything further to say. Not surprisingly, he did not. I found him guilty of the offence with which he had been charged but instead of punishing him I warned him about his future behaviour. The normal procedure then was that the principal officer would order the trainee to turn about and would march him out of the office. On this occasion I asked the principal officer to remain behind. I told him that what he had done was quite unacceptable, that I should report the incident to the governor but that I was not going to do so. He should be quite clear that I would not tolerate such behaviour from him or any other officer. He accepted the rebuke without comment.

With more experience or more confidence at the time I would have reported the matter to the governor. In the prison service of today such an incident would have been reported to the police for investigation. I was left with the feeling that the principal officer had deliberately been testing my reaction and would now simply ensure that while I was about all discipline would be enforced according to the regulations.

I remained less than convinced at the imposition of petty restrictions which bore no relation to the way ordinary people lived. Every Saturday morning the wing governor had to go round each cell to check that everything was laid out in exact order: bedclothes folded and squared to the inch; toothbrush at a forty-five-degree angle to the shoe brush; no dust on the window ledge; nothing stored under the bed. In the real world no normal person followed such an ordered way of life. It seemed to me that such an attention to unnecessary detail would only convince these young men that any form of personal order in their lives was pointless and to be avoided.

I was forcibly reminded of those Saturday mornings twelve years later when, as governor of Peterhead Prison, I was responsible for the care of those prisoners who had been labelled as the most disruptive in the Scottish prison system, men who refused to conform to any imposed discipline. Almost all of them had been known to me years before in the Allocation Centre in Polmont Borstal.

The statutory maximum for a period of borstal training at that time was two years. There was no minimum. The average period served was nine or ten months. The first six weeks were spent in the Allocation Centre. Life there was an odd mixture of bustle and boredom. When they were out of their rooms trainees were expected to do everything at great speed. But once a task had been completed there were long periods of inactivity.

The main purpose during this period was to make some form of assessment about the needs of the individual trainee and how he might benefit from the education, work and training which was available. One of the most important decisions to be made was where the period of borstal training was to take place. If the young man had no previous convictions for road traffic offences and no history of absconding from institutions he would be selected for one of two open borstals. Noranside was a former tuberculosis hospital set high above Forfar, a small country town in the northeast of Scotland, well away from the central belt of the country from which most of the young men came. There some of them would learn how to milk cows or to cut timber. Most of them spent the day sewing up shirts to be worn by prisoners. Castle Huntly was a medieval castle near Dundee which had been converted into a penal institution. Most of the young men who were sent there were given training in car mechanics and so had to show a particular aptitude for that type of work before being selected.

The vast majority of trainees served their sentences in Polmont. After six weeks in the Allocation Centre they were sent to one of the other wings and allocated to a work party. This was usually in one of the main workshops, where they would learn basic skills in light engineering or woodwork or would sew prison uniforms. For those who were thought capable, there was the possibility of a ten-week training course in car mechanics, painting and decorating or joinery. A chosen few worked in the garden party. Others worked in the kitchen or doing domestic duties around the institution.

Most trainees had the opportunity of attending part-time education. For a few of them this meant the opportunity to complete examination courses which had been interrupted when they received their custodial sentences. For many more, who had learned very little during their school days, it meant an opportunity to learn to read and to write properly. Physical activity played a large part in the routine. There was a well-equipped gymnasium, a swimming pool and generous playing fields.

Visitors were allowed to come once a month at weekends. Visits took place in one of the classrooms and visitors were encouraged to speak to staff before or after the visit.

The security of Polmont consisted of the locks on the doors of the buildings and the bars on the windows. There was no perimeter security. For the majority of prisoners this did not present a problem. They would have much preferred not to be in borstal but they accepted that there was no alternative other than to complete their sentence. For the small number who had tried to run away or who were considered to be escape risks, often on rather thin evidence, life was very different. They went to work and to education as normal, they could also use the swimming pool, since all of these facilities were linked by secure corridors, but they were not allowed outside the buildings. This meant that for the duration of their sentence, which was anything between nine and twenty-four months, they had not one breath of fresh air, other than through a window, nor did they tread on the earth. No one, to my knowledge, ever complained at this, nor was it regarded as an unacceptable deprivation.

Once they had settled to the regime trainees were given the opportunity to become involved in activities outside the institution. There was a close link between Polmont and an organization which looked after handicapped youngsters. Once or twice a year a group of staff and borstal trainees took some of these youngsters off to camp for two weeks. This experience confirmed the important fact that we generally fail to capitalize on the generosity of spirit of most human beings. For many of the borstal trainees this was the first time that they had been asked to help some people whom they regarded as being more disadvantaged than they were. They probably learned more from that experience than from the myriad of other occasions on which they were told what failures they were.

Borstal had a more positive ethos than other types of penal establishments. Many staff firmly believed that they could provide the trainees with a structure which they had never had in their lives. Trainees frequently responded to this positively. I remember one young man commenting that for the first time in his life he knew what was allowed and what was not.

In the final analysis it was asking too much that four hundred of the most difficult young men in Scotland could be brought together under one roof and be taught a different set of values and behaviour from those they had grown up with. There was a great gap in maturity between most of the sixteen-year-old youngsters who were there and those who, at the age of almost twenty-one were as mature as they would ever be. Those who were damaged and vulnerable on admission would be quickly spotted by the others and would be subjected to enormous pressure. Those who regarded themselves as hardened and mature resented being treated as 'lads' and became confirmed in their attitudes.

Dealing with such young men was a skilled task for which prison officers were given no special training. It often took superhuman patience not to respond in kind to aggressive and challenging behaviour and sometimes prison officers did not have superhuman patience. There was also a small number of staff who were quite unsuited to deal with difficult young men and who took advantage of their supervisory position. They were often men who had never worked in an adult prison. The principal officer to whom I referred above would never have dared to raise his hand to an adult prisoner.

But the major failing of the borstal system was that it did not relate the experience of imprisonment to the world from which the young men came and to which they would return. The system gave the borstal trainees very confused messages. Unattractive as the regime may have seemed to an outsider, it presented little challenge to many of those who underwent it. Perhaps for the first time in their lives the young men had a room of their own, even though the door had no handle on the inside. They had a regular life style, with reasonable food, the sheets on the bed were changed regularly. There was a swimming pool, regular access to a gym and to sports facilities. The work was boring but it was not demanding and there might be the chance to learn a bit about cars or joinery.

Many people would regard the treatment meted out by staff from time to time and by other prisoners as harsh. For a young man brought up to accept violence, even in the home, as the norm and who expected physical abuse as a response to his own violent behaviour, the odd cuff about the head or punch in the ribs was no less than he expected. It confirmed his understanding that life was all about power and that those with the greatest power exercised it through force.

What was never quite clear was what borstal trained a young man for. It took him from his own environment, gave him a new experience or perhaps confirmed previous experiences, and then sent him back into the environment from which he had come with little support when he most needed it.

It was important, for example, that young men should be kept active while they were in custody. There was a recognition that much of the work which they were required to do each day would be of little practical benefit to them on release: there was not much call for young men with sewing machine skills in the east end of Glasgow. None the less, it was important that they should learn what was known as 'the work habit' and realize that for most people the working week involves a regular routine which has to be followed each day.

What was not recognized was that, even in the late 1970s, many young men coming out of custody would not be able to find employment. One particular case springs to mind. It was of a young man who had a passion for cars. He had begun to steal them before he was eligible to have a driving licence. By the time he was old enough to drive he already had a ten-year driving ban. While in Borstal he jumped at the opportunity to be trained as a car mechanic. He turned out to be a gifted mechanic and passed his City and Guild examinations with distinction. It was clear that the best possibility of diverting him from a recurring cycle of car theft was to find him a job on release working with cars. This proved impossible despite the combined efforts of the prison service, the social work department and his local job centre. The closest he came was when the transport department of Glasgow District Council advertised for trainee mechanics. They received three thousand applications for ten vacancies. The borstal trainee was not short-listed. Within months of his release he was back in custody charged with car theft.

It was as important then as it is today to give young men like that something positive to aim for in life, to help them to realize that they had some talents to contribute to the society in which they lived. We were training them for an employment which they would never have. We should have been training them to deal constructively with unemployment. This would have involved greater opportunity to develop personal creative talent; encouragement for all of them to help people who were more disadvantaged than they were; developing skills which they could use in their lengthy leisure time.

The chasm between the experience of borstal training and the life to which the young man returned on release was underlined with stark clarity by John Steele as he described how he left Polmont at the end of his sentence:

> I was allowed home in April 1973, after serving eleven months. I said goodbye to my pals, some of whom I'd promised to keep in touch with when I got out. The warders drove us to the station and left us to catch the train into Glasgow. It was a great feeling to be free again. It was like finishing a life sentence. I said to myself the hard life was all over: regardless of what the bastards thought, I'd never be back in again.

Within six months John Steele, like so many before him and since, was back in custody.

THE YOUNG OFFENDER

The practice of holding younger prisoners apart from those who were thought to be more mature was a recognition that people are affected by the environments in which they live, and the more impressionable the person the greater the chance of being influenced. The present arrangements are based on the two premises that young people should not be sent to prison before they reach the age of sixteen years and that those who are under twenty-one years of age are by definition more impressionable than those who have reached that magic age.

The political climate in the years immediately after the end of the Second World War paved the way for the introduction of the detention centre regime for young offenders. This regime was based closely on the image of the military 'glasshouse' and the Home Secretary of the time, Chuter Ede, referred to it as 'a short, sharp shock'. He was no doubt aware that the phrase had first been used by Gilbert and Sullivan to refer to capital punishment. The regime was unashamedly deterrent and was based on military drill, physical exercise and hard work. Its main weakness was that in terms of deterrence it did not work any more efficiently than any other form of detention.

The provisions of the Criminal Justice Act 1982 abolished the sentences of borstal training and imprisonment for young offenders and were replaced by a youth custody order for those sentenced to less than three weeks or more than four months deprivation of liberty. With limited exceptions those given sentences between three weeks and four months were sent to detention centres. In 1988 the sentence of detention centre training was abolished and the generic young offender institution was introduced.

The principle of separating those who are more impressionable from those who are more mature is a sound one. To do so on the basis of age alone is too crude a criterion. It takes no account of individual rates of development. Even on the basis of chronological maturity, the gap between a young man who has just turned sixteen and another who is approaching his twenty-first birthday is likely to be significant. An establishment which holds 100, or in some cases up to 600, of the most difficult young men in our society is likely to be very volatile and is hardly likely to provide the stability needed to allow these young men to mature.

Young men in this setting can be very cruel to each other. There is an immediate tendency for the strong to prey on the relatively weak. Young offender institutions have a sorry history of self-harm, sometimes fatal, by young men who cannot cope with the pressures which they have to undergo.

In the mid 1980s in Scotland the main establishment for young offenders was at Glenochil, near Alloa. Between October 1981 and February 1984 five young men died while serving sentences there. The media regularly recorded public concern with headlines such as 'M.P. Calls for Glenochil Inspection' (*The Scotsman*, 20.8.93); 'Three Deaths Too Many' (*Sunday Mail*, 21.9.83); 'Avoiding Other Tragedies' (*The Scotsman*, 22.9.83).

Following concern expressed by the Sheriff Principal for the region, the Secretary of State for Scotland set up a working party under the chairmanship of a consultant psychiatrist 'to review the precautionary procedures adopted at Glenochil Young Offenders' Institute and Glenochil Detention Centre to identify and supervise inmates who might be regarded as suicide risks; and to make recommendations'. While the review was under way two further self-inflicted deaths took place within the complex.

The Chiswick Report[4] contained 63 recommendations. The working party took a broad view of its remit and extended its deliberations to the general regime and management at Glenochil as well as giving some thought to the criminal justice process for those under the age of twenty-one. The report stopped short of recommending the closure of Glenochil but did recommend that the establishment should be divided into smaller units, that staffing should be organized on a group basis and that each young offender should be allocated an officer who would take a particular interest in his progress.

A year or so later the reduction in the number of young men sentenced to detention following the changes brought about by the Criminal Justice (Scotland) Act 1980 meant that Glenochil was converted from a young offenders institution to an adult prison. Young offenders who had to be held in secure conditions were transferred to establishments in Dumfries and Greenock, which were much smaller and which did not suffer from the ethos which had developed in the larger establishment.

Such a conversion has not been possible at Feltham Young Offenders Institution and Remand Centre in west London.

Feltham, with 874 places, is reputed to be one of the largest complexes for young offenders in western Europe. Its buildings are relatively new, having been opened between 1983 and 1988, and its facilities are good. Despite this it has an awesome reputation.

In the preface to the report which he submitted to the Home Secretary in 1989 following an inspection of Feltham, Her Majesty's Chief Inspector of Prisons commented:

> It seems particularly unfortunate to find within the elegant and modern buildings of Feltham, so carefully landscaped, all the defects of poor regimes. Many of the boys and young men suffer from spending far too long in their cells, a lack of evening activity, and the troubles that accompany enforced idleness. [5]

Many of the troubles that accompany enforced idleness have to do with the way the young men relate to each other. Like adult prisoners, many of them will have little in common other than the fact that they have been deprived of their liberty. Some will be strong-willed and strong-minded young men, others will be immature and little more than children, many will have a very low tolerance threshold and will respond to any pressure which they experience by pressurizing those who are weaker than they.

Interviewed in *The Observer* newspaper, the governor of Feltham acknowledged:

> Bullying to the extent we have in Feltham is, I think, endemic to the whole of the young offender system. It's a product of the fact that we are not locking up 800 boy scouts: we have some of the most difficult, volatile and disturbed young men in the south of England. [6]

The extent of the bullying was brought into terrible focus at the inquest into the death of eighteen-year-old Lee Waite, who died at Feltham on 31 August 1991. Lee had been arrested on charges of car stealing and had originally been given bail. He absconded from a bail hostel and committed further offences. On 26 August he was remanded to Feltham. For the first two days he shared a cell with a friend with whom he had been arrested. After a further court appearance the friend was transferred to another young offenders institution and Lee was placed in a cell on his own. At the inquest into his death another prisoner gave evidence. He said that on the evening of 31 August he had seen two other prisoners threatening Lee. They had taken his trainers and watch. The prison officers on duty did not see this incident. The inquest heard evidence that Lee had been the subject of a much more serious assault. An autopsy revealed bruises to his buttock and lacerations to his rectum. There were reports that he had been abused with a billiard cue on his arrival by a 'kangaroo court welcoming committee'. When the night patrol officer checked Lee Waite's cell at 7.00 a.m. on 31 August he saw Lee hanging from the upturned bed. His body was cold when it was cut down. A note was found in his cell. It said, 'Please inform these people of my stupidity.' The people named were the friend with whom he had originally shared a cell, his mother and his girlfriend. [7]

In October 1991 the Inspectorate of Prisons carried out a short inspection of Feltham. They found that little had changed since their earlier visit. The local coroner wrote to the Chief Inspector following an inquest which he had carried out into the death of a fifteen-year-old youth in Feltham on 22 September 1991. He pointed out that the young man, Jeffrey Horler, who came from Great Yarmouth, had been sent to serve his sentence of 188 days in an establishment some 200 miles from his home. As a result he received no family visits and had been unable to attend the funeral of a relative. At weekends, as a juvenile, he had only two periods of daily association, one hour in the morning and two hours in the afternoon. From 4.30 p.m. each day he was locked up and isolated for some 16 hours. The coroner commented that he found the prison officers who gave evidence at the inquest to be caring and concerned, but he queried whether the regime was acceptable for a boy of this age. The governor of Feltham made his own feelings clear at the inquest:

> I personally wish to say how abhorrent it is to have to deal with children – because that is what Jeffrey was, a child – in a penal setting and under the conditions in which I have to run Feltham for want of staff. It should be totally unacceptable in this age and it indicates we are bankrupt of ideas and compassion in dealing with these admittedly very

difficult but, nevertheless, very young and very vulnerable children. [8]

Problems such as these are not confined to Feltham. There have been similar difficulties at other young offender institutions such as Glen Parva in Leicestershire.

END THOUGHTS

In 1987, when I was governor of Greenock Prison in Scotland, it was decided that the prison, which until then had held adult prisoners serving long sentences of imprisonment, should be converted into a young offenders institution. This conversion was unpopular for a variety of reasons. One was that there is a general perception among staff and, perhaps, the public that dealing with long-term adult prisoners carries much more weight and requires much more professionalism than dealing with young offenders.

The reality is in many respects quite the opposite. In most circumstances adult prisoners accept the fact of their imprisonment and wish to serve their sentences quietly and with as little fuss as possible. They may frequently attempt to outwit the staff and will try to bend regulations to their own best advantage. That is a reality which both staff and prisoners recognize and can cope with.

Young offenders are much more volatile and less cohesive. In an adult prison older prisoners will ensure that a young hothead does not disrupt the smooth running of any part of the prison for too long. This internal pressure does not exist among young offenders. Those who are more mature are likely to resent being regarded as less than adult. Those who are themselves under pressure because of being in custody are likely to compensate by exerting pressure on others. In their personal development many are still at odds with any authority and react negatively to any direction which they are given.

In such an environment staff have to show great professionalism. They require a set of skills which go far beyond any which they have been given in their training. The prison service gives no special training for those officers who work with particular groups of prisoners. There will always be a temptation when faced with a really truculent young man to react in a physical manner. In addition to being against the law, such a reaction will merely serve to confirm the young man's view of the world. Life for him is about power. He who has the greatest physical power is in charge. The only difference in a penal setting is that the staff 'gang' is stronger than the prisoner 'gang'.

One of the most depressing visits I have paid to a foreign penal establishment was made early in 1993 to the School of Re-education and Rehabilitation at Gaesti in Romania. This was in effect a prison for young people between the ages of fourteen and eighteen years. The 'school' allegedly had places for 800 youngsters although it was then holding 1200 and had recently held up to 1800. 170 of the young people were female. The maximum sentence being served was five years. Once sentenced a young person would stay in the school regardless of age. So, someone sentenced to five years just before his or her eighteenth year would remain in the school until almost twenty-three years.

The young people were housed in dormitories, each with about 65 beds in triple-tiered bunks which were crammed together. People were assigned to dormitories according to date of admission. There was no segregation according to age; the youngest lived in the same dormitory as the oldest. Most of the residents spent the majority of each day and all of each night in the dormitory. There was one member of staff for every five dormitories. Despite this, the director insisted that physical or sexual abuse was a rare occurrence. External sources painted a different story.

The young people had no personal possessions. There was no evidence of items of personal hygiene such as toothbrushes, toothpaste or soap. The heads of the young men were shaved and they all wore long, grey greatcoats. These latter were a necessary precaution against the cold since there was virtually no heating in the establishment.

The director and his senior staff gave the impression of being caring people but they were faced with an impossible task. In the culture of the country there was little concept of preparing the youngsters for a return to the community, nor of helping them to maintain and develop links with their families. We would never permit the existence of such an institution in the United Kingdom. Or would we? I thought of the conditions which had led so many young men to take their lives in Glenochil in the mid 1980s and in Feltham in the early 1990s, and of so much human misery in other penal establishments for young people around the country.

There is no doubt that some of the young people who are locked up in these establishments have committed serious crimes. Others are public nuisances. In terms of simple punishment it may be necessary to deprive them of their liberty. In respect of deterring others or of minimizing the likelihood that they will commit further crime after release, there is little sense in locking up five or six hundred of them together, often 200 or more miles from home, in establishments where the staff may be well-meaning but have little training in the extremely complex task of caring for the most difficult and unpredictable young people in society.

There must be a better way of dealing with this problem.

There is a growing body of opinion in the United Kingdom which questions the continuing relevance of retaining a segregation of prisoners based solely on the historical watershed of one's twenty-first birthday. There is a need to separate immature young people from those who are older, if not wiser. This would best be done by an assessment of individual need rather than in a blanket manner. If there has to be a division based on age it would be much better placed at eighteen years, with those under that age being subject to a welfare system which would provide both care and control.

If there is to be such a concept as individual change for those who are deprived of their liberty, it is most likely to be realized by those who are not yet set in their way of life. For such change to be effected, young people have to be treated as individuals and not in the mass. This means that they should be held together in small groups, rather than in the large anonymous establishments which we have at present.

Caring for these young people in a firm, sensitive and just manner is a highly skilled responsibility. Staff who look after them must be well trained and confident in their ability.

The young people must also be given a sense of their own worth; an understanding that they are valued members of society with something to contribute to it. This process must begin during the time that they are deprived of their liberty. It must certainly extend to their lives after release. This is not a soft option. It is a very difficult one. It is the only one which has any hope of affecting the future behaviour of these young people.

It is also the only option which meets the standard required by the United Nations Standard Minimum Rules for the Administration of Juvenile Justice:[9]

> Rule 1.4. Juvenile justice shall be conceived as an integral part of the national development process of each country, within a comprehensive framework of social justice for all juveniles, thus, at the same time, contributing to the protection of the young and the maintenance of a peaceful order in society.

REFERENCES

1. Report from the Departmental Committee on Prisons (1895), HMSO, London, Cmnd 7702.
2. Ruck, S. K. (1951), *Paterson on Prisons: Being the Collected Papers of Sir Alexander Paterson,* Frederick Muller, London.
3. Steele, J. (1992), *The Bird That Never Flew,* Sinclair-Stevenson, London.
4. Report of the Review of Suicide Preventions at HM Detention Centre and HM Young Offenders Institution Glenochil, HMSO, Edinburgh.
5. HM Chief Inspector of Prisons, Report on HM Young Offender and Remand Centre, Feltham (1989), Home Office, London.
6. *The Observer*, 22 March 1992.
7. The Howard League for Penal Reform (1993), 'Suicides in Feltham', Howard League, London.
8. *The Guardian*, 20 November 1991.
9. United Nations Standard Minimum Rules for the Administration of Juvenile Justice, adopted by the General Assembly on 29 November 1985 as an annex to Resolution 40/33.

SIX

Opportunity
and Responsibility

In 1900 a departmental report on Scottish prisons[1] recommended that a new prison should be built at Greenock, some thirty miles to the west of Glasgow, so that the prisoners from that part of the country could be kept close to their own locality and would not have to be held in prison in Glasgow. Ten years later a new prison was opened at Greenock to hold prisoners from Renfrewshire and surrounding areas. This arrangement was in keeping with the stated position of the Scottish Prison Commissioners of the time that prisoners should be kept as close as possible to their home localities.

From 1955 to the mid 1970s Greenock was the main prison in Scotland for female prisoners. It then closed for a number of years for major refurbishment and was reopened as a male prison in 1986. By that time the view expressed by the Prison Commissioners at the turn of the century was again in favour and it was decided that as far as possible the prison should be used to hold prisoners from west central Scotland. At that time there was no secure prison in the region for men serving long sentences, despite the fact that the majority of prisoners in the country came from the Greater Glasgow conurbation.

Prisons as institutions run on tradition. On being told of transfer to another establishment, even one which is many miles away, a prisoner will immediately know what to expect in the way of local rules and regulations, of staff attitudes and of the general atmosphere of the prison. The same, incidentally, will be true of staff who are similarly transferred. Once these local traditions are set, for better or for worse, it requires a great deal of effort and commitment to change them.

The opportunity is provided with a new prison to set new traditions, to establish new priorities, to introduce a new set of human relationships. There is a window of opportunity, lasting no more than a year, in which this can be achieved. This is a time of great challenge and of great danger. Given that the majority of staff and of prisoners will have come from other prisons, they will bring their old ways of working and living with them. 'This is the way we did it in . . .' Both groups know from their respective positions that once traditions are set they will be hard to change. It is, therefore, important in the early months of any new prison to set the parameters according to one's own perspective. One might expect prisoners to push hard to extend them as far as possible while staff might wish to keep them as restricted as possible.

In 1986 Greenock was the first new prison for adult male prisoners to be opened in Scotland for 60 years. At that time a new philosophy of imprisonment was beginning to find practical expression. The paternalistic notion of rehabilitation as something which could be imposed on another person had been recognized as being unsound both in theory and in practice. It was unsound in theory because of the arrogance in the assumption that one group of human beings could impose personal change on another group of human beings. It was unsound in practice because it simply did not work. Internal change in a human being cannot be imposed from outside. These realities had led to the discrediting of the notion of rehabilitation.

It was all very well to argue that the traditional concept of imprisonment had been discredited. But it was not sufficient to dismiss imprisonment as a completely negative experience. It was necessary to develop a new framework; one which could be understood by all participants in the debate: politicians, academics, the public and especially by prisoners and prison staff.

Such a framework begins with a recognition of the reality of custody. A prisoner is required to complete the sentence which has been passed by the court. This fact is not negotiable and cannot be altered. The reality of this has always been recognized by prisoners and by prison personnel. The prisoner sees the bars on the cell window and notices that there is no handle on the inside of the cell door. The officer knows that his or her primary duty is to lock up in the evening the same number of men or women who were unlocked in the morning.

There is also an obligation to maintain good order within prisons. One consequence of the requirement of custody is that the prison is a coercive institution in which one group of people deprives another group of people of their liberty. This coercion inevitably leads to a tension, but it is a tension which need not necessarily be destructive. The good order which is necessary in a prison implies much more than control. It involves a set of relationships which ensure a safe working environment for staff and a safe living environment for prisoners.

Finally, this framework will take account of the obligation placed on the system to offer prisoners the opportunity to spend their time in prison constructively and to prepare themselves for release. The concept of 'opportunity' is a recognition that in respect of re-habilitation, that is, of personal change from within, the prisoner is master of his or her own destiny. He or she is a human being, with a free will, with rights and with responsibilities. The need is to give the prisoner, and for him or her to take, as much respon-sibility as possible for his or her own life and actions.

The opening of Greenock Prison provided an opportunity to put these principles into practice. The majority of the staff were in post before the prisoners arrived and were encouraged to draw up a framework for a regime which was to be based on mutual respect between staff and prisoners. Named staff were to provide support for groups of prisoners. Prisoners were to be encouraged to discuss their progress and plans for the future with these members of staff. They were to see the reports which were to be written about them. Regular access to families and friends through correspondence and visits and by telephone was to be a key feature of the prison. This would be aided by the fact that the families of most of the prisoners would live within easy travelling distance of the prison.

In April 1986, six weeks after it opened, I was appointed as Governor of Greenock Prison.

THE GOVERNOR'S TALE

If a society decides that it has to have prisons, an establishment such as Gateside Prison at Greenock would be a good model. It is in an urban area, close to the community which it serves. It has two accommodation blocks, with 130 and 50 cells respectively. When it reopened in 1986 pressure on prison accommodation in the country as a whole was such that it was decided that there should be two prisoners to a cell in the smaller hall, giving a total population of 230 prisoners. All cells have a toilet and a washbasin. Each accommodation hall has its own dining room, which doubles as a recreation room. There is a reasonably sized visiting room, an education unit, a medical centre, a chapel which is used for a variety of activities, industrial work shops and a sports field.

There were 100 uniformed officers and 30 other staff. Great emphasis was placed on the need for all staff to work as a team rather than in individual units. The structure of accountability was based on delegation of responsibility to the lowest appropriate level in any given circumstance. This format had two main elements. On the part of senior staff it required self-discipline not to become involved in matters which had been delegated and it also required trust that junior staff were capable of carrying out the duties which had been delegated to them provided they were properly supported. It required junior staff to feel confident of their own abilities and also to recognize when a matter was outside their bounds of competence and needed be referred elsewhere.

Given that all the prisoners were serving long sentences, there was comparatively little turnover. This gave staff and prisoners an opportunity to get to know each other. This was particularly important in the early days when both groups were testing each other out, often with memories of encounters in other prisons. Following a consistent lead from senior management, both staff and prisoners eventually recognized that treating each other decently and with civility need not threaten their respective positions. Staff learned that by getting to know prisoners as people they did not place security at risk. On the contrary, they were more likely to sense trouble before it arose and to prevent it instead of having to deal with it after it had surfaced. It was also more difficult for a prisoner to attack verbally or physically an officer with whom he was on first-name terms. Once they became confident about what they were doing staff also gained greater job satisfaction from their work. Levels of sick absence were low and officers became involved in many additional activities.

Prisoners learned that living in this way made their sentences more bearable and removed the need for constant posturing. Not that it was an easy option. One old lag, who had spent upwards of thirty years in prison, found it impossible to settle to this new way of living and demanded to be sent back to a more traditional regime in Barlinnie Prison in Glasgow. He later wrote to me to explain why he could not settle. He encouraged me to continue with my 'progressive policies' and regretted the fact that he was not thirty years younger! Another prisoner, serving a life sentence, who had come to Greenock direct from the punishment cells in Peterhead left after sixteen months to go to the Barlinnie Special Unit. On leaving, he told me that his spell in Greenock had been the most rewarding but also personally the most difficult of his many years in prison.

There were many cameos played out which demonstrated a significant degree of insight into what was happening. One of several officers who had come from Peterhead Prison found it particularly difficult to settle and was very slow to establish any sort of relationship with prisoners. There was one experienced prisoner on his gallery who had served time previously in Peterhead but who had come to Greenock from Perth Prison. One evening the officer was in his usual place on the bridge of the landing with a newspaper spread out in front of him which was his way of letting prisoners know that he did not want to be disturbed. The prisoner took up position some yards away and began to stare directly at the officer. At first the officer tried to ignore him but as minutes passed he became quite uneasy. Eventually he could take it no longer.

'What do you want, then?' he demanded.

The prisoner continued to look him in the eye and replied, 'You know, I've been watching you and it's not true what they say about you.'

The officer could not resist.

'What do they say about me?'

'That you're just a crotchety old bastard.'

The other staff and prisoners who had surreptitiously been watching this ceremony exploded with laughter. The officer in question never quite became the prisoners' friend but he softened noticeably after this exchange.

Prisoners were unlocked at 6.30 each weekday morning. With the exception of short periods when they were locked up for roll checks, they could remain out of their cells until 9.00 p.m. At weekends the day lasted from 7.30 a.m. until 5.00 p.m. The three meals of the day were eaten in the dining room. From 8.00 a.m, until noon and from 1.30 until 4.30 p.m. prisoners were at work. Most of them worked in either the joinery or the textile workshop. Others carried out various maintenance or housekeeping tasks around the prison.

Men were encouraged to spend some time each week in the education unit. This was staffed by two full-time teachers and a number of part-timers from the local college of further education. The prison had a contract with the college to reimburse all the costs involved. A similar arrangement applied in most prisons in the United Kingdom at the time. It was ideal in that it provided the prison with a regular teaching staff but also allowed access to the facilities of the local college. It also ensured that the teachers did not lose contact with progress in the field of wider education.

Classes offered included English, history, art, mathematics and arithmetic at national examination level as well as computing, sociology, basic numeracy and drama. There were also opportunities for individual study in other subjects. Many of the prisoners had no more than irregular schooling when they were young. The level of achievement was low in most cases and the level of unrealized potential was high. It was a sad statement of fact that many of them had to come to prison to learn to read and to write. To be able to do so and to go on to higher studies gave them an important sense of their own worth, in some cases a realization of unknown potential and the possibility of making something positive of their future.

As in many prisons the products of the art classes filled what would otherwise have been dreary institutional corridors. The majority of the work was of soaring eagles or rampaging elephants but here and there one came across an indication of real artistic talent. The quarterly prison magazine was another vehicle for unexpected creativity.

Close by the workshops was an activity hall and a multi-gym area. There was also a small all-weather football pitch. A full range of sports was available along with fitness and weight training.

On weekday evenings and at weekends prisoners had free time which could be spent on the table tennis or snooker tables which were on the ground floor of the accommodation halls or in the dining rooms where there were table games, television and reading materials.

There were part-time Church of Scotland and Catholic chaplains who both conducted Sunday services and who visited regularly during the week to carry out pastoral duties. Arrangements were made for clergymen of other denominations to visit prisoners as necessary.

The prison was served by a local medical practice. A doctor from this practice visited the prison each morning and at other times as necessary to treat those who were ill. Other specialists, including a dentist, a psychiatrist and a psychologist visited on a regular basis.

Showers were available in each hall and could be used by prisoners on a daily basis. Prisoners were issued with enough personal kit to allow for three changes of socks and of underwear each week.

The prison had a full-time social worker. As with most of the other specialist workers, she was on secondment from the local authority, an arrangement which allowed all of them to maintain a degree of independence from the establishment. She would see all prisoners who had asked to see her or who were referred by gallery officers. She also acted as a resource point and consultant for the prison officers in carrying out their expanded role.

Representatives of voluntary and statutory agencies came into the prison regularly to help prisoners with a wide range of problems such as drug and alcohol abuse, future employment and accommodation.

One is conscious in describing the range of activities which were available in Greenock Prison that the reader who has no knowledge of prison might well conclude that there is little or no punishment in such a model of imprisonment. A person is hardly likely to be deterred from a life of crime by an experience which bears a remarkable resemblance to a traditional boarding school and which compares favourably to service in the armed forces.

The reality is somewhat different. However decent the conditions of imprisonment, however positive the experiences which are offered, the prisoner is always acutely conscious of deprivation of liberty. The cell door closes each night. Barring life and death emergencies, it will not be opened until next morning.

When a person walks through the gateway of a prison virtually all responsibility and ability to exercise personal initiative is taken from him or her. One has to live one's life at the behest of other people. Every moment of one's day is charted in advance. It will be the same tomorrow, next week, next year.

One of the greatest pains of imprisonment for most people is separation from family and friends. This was true at Greenock Prison where the arrangements for maintaining contact compared favourably with many other prisons. Prisoners were allowed to write and to receive unlimited letters. At that time all letters were censored. This process has now ceased for all but prisoners in the highest security category.

Visits from family and friends took place on weekday evenings and on afternoons at weekends and lasted for sixty minutes. Prisoners were guaranteed a minimum of two visits each month but in practice were able to have more. Visits took place around small tables in an open room. Drinks and snacks were available and there was a small play area for children.

Greenock was one of the first prisons in the United Kingdom in which prisoners had access to pay telephones. Prisoners are paid a few pounds each week for the daily work which they do. In Greenock payment was made in cash. In most other prisons payment is through a credit system. The homes of most prisoners were within a fifty-mile radius of the prison and many of them got into the habit of making a short call home each evening at cheap rate. The telephones could not receive incoming calls.

Even this apparently positive development was not without its consequences. In the course of a discussion one afternoon a prisoner described the effect regular telephone contact had on his relations with his family. He explained how visits twice a month with his wife could be passed discussing 'safe' subjects such as the weather, the state of the economy and the prospects for the local football team. They never really got down to discussing family matters which were important to both of them. This was an unacknowledged method of coping with the pains of separation. However, this man went on, now that he was in the habit of speaking to his wife every day they had begun to discuss topics which had previously been avoided: the teenage daughter who stayed out until the small hours of the morning, the son who was truanting from school. The father felt himself much closer to his family than he had before but at the same time he was frustrated at his inability to exert any influence. The man did not present this as an argument against the provision of pay telephones. He was simply pointing out that it was wrong to assume that it solved all the problems of separation from family.

Prisons are not intended primarily to turn people who have committed crimes into men and women who will contribute positively to society. That task is much better carried out in the community. However, there is a tradition in many prisons of involvement in the local community in a manner which benefits the community and which encourages those in custody to help others who are less fortunate than themselves. This can be done by allowing men and women who do not present a significant risk to the public to help in places such as old people's homes or to work with handicapped people. In high security prisons the option may be to bring the community into the prison. At Greenock prisoners developed the practice of entertaining groups of senior citizens and of handicapped youngsters regularly throughout the year.

COPING WITH CHANGE

There are certain dates in one's life which are never forgotten. 11 February 1987 is one such for me. I arrived at Greenock Prison shortly before eight o'clock to be met by the chief officer, who told me that the prisoners were sitting quietly in the dining rooms, refusing to move. The local radio had been playing during the breakfast period. The 7.30 news had carried an item that Greenock Prison was to be turned into a young offenders institution and the adult prisoners were all to be transferred to the new high security prison at Shotts. I had been aware that this change was being considered but did not know that any decision had been made. I certainly was not expecting a public announcement in this fashion. The prisoners were understandably irate at the news and at the manner in which they had heard it.

There was only one way to handle the situation. Along with the chief officer I went to the main dining room. I told the men that they knew more about the situation than I did. I said that I would go to Edinburgh to see the Director of Prisons and seek clarification. I would then return to bring them up to date. In the meantime, the best thing they could do was to get on with their normal day's work. I held my breath . . . After what seemed an interminable pause one or two prisoners rose, to be followed by others. All went to work. On that day we called in much of the good will which had been built up in the previous year.

In the course of the 1980s there had been a significant reduction in the number of young men under the age of 21 years, young offenders, sentenced to custody. During the same period there had been a significant increase in the adult prison population, particularly among those sentenced to long periods of imprisonment. These two facts had resulted in an underuse of the accommodation for young offenders and considerable overcrowding in some adult prisons. In order to redress this balance it had been suggested that the large young offenders institution at Glenochil might be used as an adult prison and that Greenock might become a young offenders institution. It was envisaged that these changes might take effect later in 1987 when the new prison at Shotts became available.

In the course of my visit to Edinburgh I learned that no final decision had been made. The media had heard of the plans which were being considered and had broadcast them. That left us in a dangerous position. The prisoners were told that the change might indeed happen but that the matter had not yet been decided. They were encouraged to continue as normal and to give no ammunition to those who were waiting for things to go wrong.

The final decision that this change should happen was made in May 1987 and the transfer of prisoners began the following month. The intervening period was very unsettling for both staff and prisoners. The latter had shown a great deal of trust in cooperating in the development of the new regime and now felt that this trust had been abused. Staff felt that their contribution had counted for nothing.

Over a period of some four weeks in June and July 1987 about 1500 men, over 25 per cent of the prisoners in Scotland, were transferred to different establishments. In the short term all went well. The transfers were effected without major disruption. In the longer term, it is hard to evaluate the extent to which the riots and hostage-taking which occurred across Scottish prisons between the autumn of 1987 and 1990 were influenced by the instability engendered by the disruption caused in the wake of so many transfers.

Shotts Prison had been opened in 1978. Between then and 1981 I had been its first deputy governor. The original intention had been that it would hold 1000 prisoners. In the event it opened with capacity for only 60 prisoners. A 1978 departmental inquiry into United Kingdom prisons[2] described it as a 'truncated monster' and recommended that it should be expanded considerably.

The expansion, which was in effect a new prison with a total of 528 places, was not completed until the summer of 1987. It was to become the main prison in Scotland for adult male prisoners serving long sentences of imprisonment. The living accommodation consisted of four main wings which were subdivided into units of twenty. All prisoners had their own cells, which included a toilet and a washbasin. Each of the four halls had a dining room and generous activity rooms. The modern facilities included industrial workshops and training shops, a well-equipped education unit, a first-class gymnasium, a chapel, a large visiting room and a small hospital. In short, the physical conditions were all that one might hope for in a prison. The lesson was to be quickly learned that there is more to a prison than good physical conditions.

During the four-week period described above, some 400 long-term prisoners were transferred to Shotts Prison from various prisons throughout Scotland. Many of them, including those from Greenock, came reluctantly. They had been settled in their previous establishments. They did not accept the need for their transfer and were not impressed by the prospect of improved physical conditions.

Many of the staff were relatively new to the prison service. For the others, Shotts was not a particularly popular posting. Like the prisoners, staff were all too conscious that the prison was in what they and their families regarded as an isolated location with very difficult access by public transport.

The challenges which had been faced in establishing Greenock as a new prison were magnified several times in Shotts. There were almost three times as many prisoners and a proportionately larger number of staff. Few in either group were immediately enthusiastic about their enforced transfers. The need to resolve the problem of overcrowding throughout the prison system meant that the prison had to be brought up to capacity much sooner than was wise. The opportunity to develop a local tradition and culture which would see the prison through difficult times was minimal. Under such pressure the management team found themselves reacting to the problems of the day rather than steering a firm course which would eventually take the establishment to where they wanted it to be.

During the first traumatic months in the life of the establishment there were several periods of disruption. These served only to make people take up traditional positions. Staff felt vulnerable. As a result they were unwilling to take what they considered to be risks in dealing with prisoners. Relationships became strained. Formality became the order of the day.

From the prisoners' perspective their worst fears were being realized. They had been given relatively good physical conditions but were being looked after by a staff who equated good order with control. The coercive features of imprisonment came to the surface and the old 'them and us' scenario reasserted itself.

There was an additional element of pressure on the new Shotts Prison. For many years the prison at Peterhead had been subject to much criticism because of its relatively isolated location, the state of its buildings and the nature of its regime. It was envisaged that in due course Shotts Prison would replace Peterhead as the major high security prison for Scotland. This decision had been implemented in fact because of the decision, which is described in the next chapter, to hold a small number of prisoners who were presenting the greatest difficulty to management in Peterhead. In effect Shotts was being asked to take on the role which Peterhead had previously carried out.

JUSTICE AND MUTUAL RESPECT: MYTH OR REALITY?

I came to Shotts Prison at the end of April 1990 with a firm belief, which had been refined in the furnace of Peterhead Prison, that no prison, but particularly one holding prisoners serving long sentences for serious crimes, could be properly managed on a foundation of fear and coercion. This was not a matter of being 'liberal' or 'progressive'. It was a matter of principle and of good management. The regime in Peterhead had been an extreme example of what happens when the 'legitimate' force of the system meets the 'illegitimate' force of the prisoners: continual confrontation and a form of naked coercion in which there were no winners. It was an environment in which good order was lacking and in which everyone, staff and prisoners, were in fear for their physical safety.

If a prison is not to be a place of anarchy and chaos there must be a sense of justice, of decency, of fairness and of consistency. These principles must apply to and be exercised by everyone who lives and works in the prison. Such a set of objectives are simply stated but require maximum commitment if they are to be realized.

The understandable response of the staff at Shotts, after a period of major disruption and an incident in which an officer had been taken hostage, had been to set up physical and psychological barriers between themselves and the prisoners. Each section of twenty cells was separated from the main section of the accommodation hall by a grille gate. In the planning process it had been envisaged that these grille gates would only ever be closed in the course of a major incident. In practice, they were closed all the time. The prisoners were allowed to circulate on their side; staff remained on the other. These grille gates had become symbolic of the divide between officers and prisoners.

A dual strategy was required if normality was to be restored. In the first place staff had to be convinced that their safety was more likely to be assured if the prisoners were kept active and lived as normal a life as possible. Officers were also more likely to be able to prevent trouble if they moved among prisoners rather than if they stood apart from them. It had to be emphasized that the great majority of prisoners wished to serve their sentence peaceably and were prepared to observe legitimate restrictions which were placed on them. If a small number of prisoners caused disruption, their individual freedom of movement within the prison would have to be restricted. But it was important not to extend these restrictions to other prisoners who were not involved.

The second part of the strategy was equally important. Prisoners had to be convinced that it was in their interests to serve their sentences in as positive a manner as possible. The reasonable requirements of security and good order were a prerequisite for that to happen. Since all the prisoners in Shotts were serving long sentences, they had to be given personal short-term targets which would give them something to aim for over a two- or three-year period. These might be to do with work skills, with educational achievements, with moving on to another prison or with personal development. These targets would only mean anything if they were agreed with the prisoner and he had commitment to them.

It was also important that as far as possible the normal courtesies of life should be observed. Put simply, people should be expected to act decently towards each other, whatever the style of their uniform. In prison the use of illegitimate power is never restricted to one side. In some prison systems brutality by staff to prisoners is institutionalized. In other systems it is formally prohibited but is none the less exercised in an informal but systematic manner. This may well occur when staff regard prisoners as acting provocatively and do not feel that management is providing them with proper protection. In its evidence[3] to the Committee on the Prison Disciplinary System[4] in 1984 the Prison Officers Association, which represents uniformed prison staff in England and Wales, made reference to the 'alternative disciplinary system':

> One possible consequence – one that we deprecate – will be to drive the disciplinary system 'underground' . . . We can see something of this happening now and it is a disaster for our service. It will destroy the morale of the prison population and make prisons even more dangerous places for prison officers to work in.

There had to be a clear message that Shotts Prison was going to be a place in which no one, staff or prisoner, would be at risk of physical harm. Within the first week or so of my arrival I had spelled this message out personally to various staff groups. Experienced officers understood the truth of what was being said. There was a large number of officers who had recently been recruited to the prison service and who knew nothing other than the regime which had developed at Shotts. They had to accept that it was not normal practice in a prison for staff to outnumber prisoners in any one location; that being a prison officer is a demanding job and one which requires confidence of approach and a degree of sensible risk-taking. It was emphasized that fulfilling and active regimes in a prison are an aid to good order rather than a threat.

I also spoke directly to the prisoners as a body in each of the four accommodation blocks. In taking this approach, a clear message was being passed to the more doubting members of staff that prisoners could be brought together and be dealt with face to face without the danger of a major riot. There was a slight element of risk in this strategy since most of the prisoners had been held in very restricted conditions for some considerable time and were likely to take up an aggressive stance. In the event there was a series of lively and forceful exchanges of view, with a mutual recognition that neither the staff nor the prisoners were free from responsibility for what had happened.

GOOD POLICIES, GOOD PRISONS?

Having laid out the foundation for the future of the prison, the main task was to begin to implement in practical terms the policies which were in the process of being set out in various documents which, for the first time, attempted to lay down comprehensive policies for the positive treatment of prisoners. The first of these, and the one which set the standard for future documents, was 'Custody and Care'.[5] Published in January 1988, it was in effect a statement of the principles which had been implemented at Greenock Prison. It introduced the notion of corporate planning for establishments. It laid out a framework for agreeing with each prisoner a plan for getting through his or her sentence. It introduced a new vocabulary which was enabling rather than prescriptive and which included such verbs as 'provide', 'promote', and 'encourage'. Like all subsequent consultative documents it was circulated widely in a consultative form before taking its final shape.

In 1990 'Opportunity and Responsibility' was published.[6] This dealt with the management of prisoners who were serving long sentences and contained a blueprint for much of what had to be done at Shotts Prison. In his introduction the Secretary of State for Scotland set the scene:

> The Government's penal policy is that the prison sentence should be imposed upon those, and only those, for whom an alternative disposal is not appropriate. But we are also concerned that, so far as is consistent with the deprivation of liberty and the protection of the

public, the disruption to family ties and work prospects, consequent upon a sentence of imprisonment, should be minimized, and the prisoner should be given opportunities to address his offending behaviour and to contribute positively to society on discharge.

The Secretary of State went on to provide a new statement of the principle of rehabilitation:

It is clear that the old objectives of 'treatment and training' are outmoded. A new approach is required, which will recognize the mutual responsibilities of the prisoner and the prison authorities and ensure that the long-term prisoner is encouraged to address his offending behaviour and offered an appropriate range of opportunities to use his time in prison responsibly for personal development.

This document broke new ground in penal policy in the United Kingdom and was available to the Woolf Inquiry when it was set up a few months later. It considered the prisoner as a person who must be encouraged to retain a sense of responsibility and be given the opportunity for personal development. It emphasized the need to lessen the harmful effects of imprisonment and to provide a basic quality of life in prison. It recognized the need to promote the prisoner's self-respect and self-esteem, particularly by improving access to families and by enabling prisoners to exercise a degree of responsible choice over how they planned their sentence.

By the beginning of the 1990s a great deal of work had been done in the Scottish prison service in laying out policy, in setting up structures, in building links and in establishing pockets of good practice. The challenge which then faced the system was to maintain this momentum and to translate it into practice in all establishments. Agreeing and publishing a coherent policy for the prison system was a courageous step for both politicians and administrators. But that was the easy part. The difficult part will be to apply that policy in a manner which meets the needs of security and good order, while also giving the prisoner the opportunity to use the time in prison positively. If this can be achieved the prisoner will be less damaged by the experience of imprisonment and will be more likely to contribute to society on release.

REFERENCES

1. Report from the Departmental Committee on Scottish Prisons (1900), HMSO, London, Cmnd 218.
2. Report of the Committee of Inquiry into the United Kingdom Prison Services (1979), HMSO, London, Cmnd 7673.
3. Prison Officers' Association (1984), 'The Prison Disciplinary System, Submissions to the Home Office Departmental Committee on the Prison Disciplinary System', Hemstal Press, London.
4. Report of The Committee on the Prison Disciplinary System (1985), HMSO, London, Cmnd 9641.
5. Scottish Prison Service (1988), 'Custody and Care: Policy and Plans for the Scottish Prison Service', HMSO, Edinburgh.
6. Scottish Prison Service (1990), 'Opportunity and Responsibility: Developing New Approaches to the Management of the Long-term Prison System in Scotland', HMSO, Edinburgh.

SEVEN

Bad Prisoners or
Bad Management?

Between November 1986 and October 1987 there was an unprecedented series of hostage-taking incidents in Scottish prisons. In most of these incidents a group of prisoners took a number of staff or prisoners hostage in a main accommodation block. Staff were forced to leave the block, which was then systematically destroyed. The most public of these incidents took place in Peterhead Prison in autumn 1987. For five days prisoners led a prison officer across the roof of an accommodation block in Peterhead Prison with a chain around his neck like a tame animal.

The governor of the prison eventually handed over management of the incident to the police and it was brought to an end by physical intervention in which the prisoners were overpowered and the prison officer was released physically unharmed. Prisoners and others believed that the intervention team had been made up of members of the Special Air Services. Official sources refused to confirm or deny this. In January 1993 one of the prisoners involved unsuccessfully sued the Secretary of State for Scotland, claiming that he had been beaten up by members of the SAS. During the hearing evidence was given by members of the SAS, which confirmed that they had indeed been involved.

At the end of 1987 there was a real fear that the whole structure of the Scottish prison system might collapse. There had been major disruption at all of the largest adult male prisons: Edinburgh, Barlinnie, Perth, Shotts and Peterhead. There was a belief that these incidents were being orchestrated with the precise aim of bringing the system to its knees.

A decision was taken to segregate those prisoners who were thought to be at the centre of the unrest and to hold them all in Peterhead Prison. If this was done, so the argument went, other prisons would be able to return to a semblance of normality. The irony of this decision was that much of the unrest in other prisons had focused on complaints about the treatment of prisoners in Peterhead.

The main body of prisoners, with the exception of a small number who were held there protected from other prisoners, had been transferred out of Peterhead after the riot which ended in early October 1987. Those who remained consisted of the eighteen or so who had taken part in riots and hostage-taking either in Peterhead or in other prisons, as well as a number who happened to have been kept there as much by chance as anything else. To this group were added a handful of men who were alleged to have been 'violent or subversive' in other prisons. The total number was about sixty. They were labelled as the most dangerous men in the Scottish prison system. They were to be held under the provisions of Prison Rule 36, that is, they were to be kept in virtual isolation, allowed no contact with each other, dealt with at all times individually by no less than three members of staff. These officers wore riot helmets and body armour and usually carried perspex shields. In order to make the prison viable, men who were kept in protected conditions in other prisons were transferred to Peterhead, bringing the total number in the prison to about 130.

In May 1988 I was asked to take over as Governor of Peterhead Prison.

THE HATE FACTORY

Shortly after the Scottish Prison Commissioners took up office in 1877 they drew attention to the fact that, because there was no convict prison in Scotland, all Scottish convicts were sent to serve their sentences in English prisons. The Commissioners objected to the fact that, while Scotland contributed its share to maintaining these convicts, the benefits of this outlay, including the public work done by convicts on harbours and elsewhere, was enjoyed by England.

This pragmatic argument gained a great deal of popular support and it was suggested that Scottish convicts might very usefully be employed on constructing a harbour of refuge somewhere on the east coast of the country. A parliamentary sub committee narrowed the choice of location to Montrose or Peterhead and eventually settled on the latter town. There was then a debate about whether the prison should be built at the spot where the harbour was to be constructed or at the granite quarry, which was about a mile away. It was concluded that the prison should be built on the coast and that the convicts should be taken to the quarry each day by private train and under armed guard.

So it happened that Scotland's one and only convict prison came to be built on a bleak headland in the northeast of Scotland, where it was exposed to all the rigours of North Sea weather. It received its first prisoners in August 1888.

It was ironic that the justification for building the prison in such a location should be what in effect was a community project, the construction of a breakwater at the harbour. In due course the local fishermen of Peterhead would benefit immensely from this project. The prisoners felt no such sense of gain. Most of them came from the Edinburgh-Glasgow conurbation, the central belt of the country in which most of the population was and still is concentrated. They had little in common with their guardians, who came from the fishing and farming communities of Aberdeenshire.

The cultural gulf between the keepers and the kept was to be an important element in the lack of understanding and sympathy between the two groups which became endemic in the following one hundred years. I fell foul of this myself shortly after taking up post at Peterhead in 1988. While attending a function in the town one of the local worthies asked me how I enjoyed living in the area. Unthinkingly, I said, 'Well, it's a bit far away.' That thoughtless comment deserved the speedy response which it engendered, 'That depends where you're coming from.'

In this respect Peterhead is similar to many maximum security prisons across the world. They are frequently built in relatively remote areas and recruit local staff who have little in common with the prisoners, who will typically come from distant centres of population. Dartmoor Prison in England springs to mind. One is also very consious of this divide when visiting, for example, Attica

State Prison in New York. The vast majority of the thousands of prisoners who are held there are young black men who have grown up in an urban environment in New York City. Their guards come predominantly from white upstate farming stock. It is a hard enough task for prisoners and prison staff to communicate at the best of times. It becomes almost impossible when there is such a wide cultural divide.

The unique role of Peterhead as a convict prison and the distance which it took prisoners from their homes set it apart from all other Scottish prisons from the time it was opened. This sense of being apart was reinforced over the years. It was the only Scottish prison in which officers carried cutlasses and those who escorted the prisoners to daily work in the granite quarry had rifles. No prisoner was allowed to come closer than a drawn cutlass-lengh to an officer. The cutlasses were withdrawn from use, very much against the wishes of the staff, in 1938.

The rifles were not ornamental. In 1932 three prisoners attempted to escape from the prison yard. One of them was shot and killed by a guard. The jury at a subsequent Fatal Accident Inquiry concluded that the officer had fired in the ordinary execution of his duties.[1] Guards at the prison quarry carried rifles until 1959.

The distinction between ordinary prisoners and convicts was finally abolished in 1949.[2] The distinct status of Peterhead in the mythology of Scottish prisons was much more difficult to eradicate. In the years after the Second World War the received wisdom in the prison systems in the United Kingdom was that prisoners who had been sentenced to more than a short time in prison should be 'trained'. Training, like the concept of dressage on which it was based, was imposed on the prisoner. It involved a regular work habit, some basic work skills and, for some, a degree of education. This form of training assumed that the prisoner was prepared to cooperate with this regime. If he was not prepared to do so, the prisoner was described as 'untrainable'. Within the Scottish prison system all untrainable prisoners were sent to Peterhead.

The consequence was that Peterhead Prison became a lethal cocktail. The prisoners held there were the least likely to conform to what the system expected of them. They fed off each other in their opposition to authority. In the terrible hierarchy of criminal labelling young men who had progressed through approved schools, borstals and young offender institutions saw Peterhead as the apex of their criminal education. They knew that if they refused to cooperate with assessment at the start of their sentences they would be labelled 'untrainable' and be sent to Peterhead. To their number was added a handful of prisoners who had been convicted of particularly high-profile crimes and who had received very long sentences. Even though they might never have been in prison previously they were sent to Peterhead since it was considered to be the most secure prison in the country.

The cavernous granite buildings were damp, ill-heated and inhospitable. There were very few facilities, such as dining, education or recreation rooms. The worksheds were in what was known as the Admiralty Yard, reached by an extended march along the exposed 'Burma Road'. A disused chimney reached skywards from one of the sheds. If its top was shrouded in mist when the chief officer looked out from the main prison in the morning the prisoners would not go to work. Much of the work involved making nets or heavy hawsers for local fishing boats, work unlikely to be of much use to prisoners when they returned to their urban communities and which merely served to underline the exiled nature of their existence.

This exile did not merely affect the prisoners. Coming from Glasgow to visit 'her man' a woman, perhaps with one or two small children in tow, would leave home at the crack of dawn to make a two-hour train journey to Aberdeen. She would then catch a bus which would take a further hour to get to Peterhead. The visiting facilities in the prison were primitive. She would go to a cramped toilet to smarten herself up and to attend to the children's needs. The visit, which would last for about two hours, took place in a bare room, more often than not with the partners separated from each other by a glass screen. When the monthly visit had ended she would retrace her long journey home. The prisoner would return to his cell, conscious of the marathon which his partner had to endure, frustrated at the lack of any real contact, waiting for a wrong word to be said by another prisoner or an officer to which he might violently respond.

This sense of being apart was not confined to the prisoners. Peterhead, its prisoners and its staff were held at arm's length by the rest of the prison system. Most of the prison officers had little in common with the prisoners. They knew that they were carrying out a task which none of their colleagues in other prisons wished to take on, yet their very location made them unknown. Visitors to Peterhead were few and far between.

The symbiotic relationship between officers and prisoners was complex. At one level there was complete antipathy, them and us, beat or be beaten. At another level there was a degree of collusion which was born of a mutual need to survive. It might manifest itself in an officer turning a blind eye to what prisoners did to each other. Prisoners would also exert an informal discipline over those among them who were most unruly to ensure that a degree of stability was maintained. Staff and prisoners reached daily accommodations which paid little more than lip service to official rules and regulations.

In such an unforgiving and harsh environment any sign of emotion or caring was interpreted as weakness. Whatever men might feel in the silence of their cells, bravado was the only face which was to be shown in public. This bravado was frequently expressed in terms of physical violence. A disagreement between staff and prisoner, prisoner and staff or prisoner and prisoner was expected to end in an explosion of power.

Over the years Peterhead became a byword for coercion. The report published in 1987 by the Gateway Exchange[3] drew attention to the fact that official statistics show that prisoners at Peterhead in the decades from the 1920s onwards consistently received more punishments per head of the prison population than in any other male prison in Scotland.

During the last thirty years there has been a tragic roll call of serious incidents in the prison. These have included riots, escapes, assaults and hostage-takings. The years between 1984 and 1987 were particularly troublesome. In 1984 there was a rooftop hostage incident. The following year staff were taken hostage in the tailors' workshop. In the same year prisoners broke out of the punishment cells and attempted to escape. The worst incident was another rooftop hostage incident in late autumn 1987. If prisoners were involved in major incidents in other prisons they were invariably transferred to Peterhead. If they became involved in similar incidents in Peterhead there was no further onward allocation, other than for a short period. In that respect Peterhead was the end of the line.

Those prisoners who were the least willing to conform were dealt with in a manner which became increasingly coercive as their acts of indiscipline continued. Those who were considered to pose the greatest threat to the public if they were to escape were placed in security category A. They were kept together at all times in what was known as the security party and subjected to the strictest supervision.

Serious acts of indiscipline were referred by the governor to the visiting committee, a group of about a dozen individuals appointed by local authorities. The most severe punishment available to a visiting committee was forfeiture of the one third remission of sentence to which a prisoner looked forward. Unlike their English counterparts, the boards of visitors, there was no limit to the amount of remission which a visiting committee could withdraw for any one offence. In the early 1980s the Peterhead visiting committee, faced with prisoners charged with what amounted to criminal offences of actual or attempted prison-breaking, rioting and assaults, awarded punishments which were in some instances greater, in terms of additional time to be spent in prison, than were available in sheriff courts. The point to be remembered was that these disciplinary hearings were not courts of law but were administrative proceedings. Concern within the Scottish Office at this course of action led in 1984 to an administrative withdrawal of the facility given to governors to refer disciplinary hearings to visiting committees.

Acts of indiscipline which appeared to be breaches of the criminal law were referred to the courts, which were severe in the punishment of serving prisoners convicted of offences committed while in prison. It was not uncommon to come across a prisoner in Peterhead who had begun his sentence facing five or six years in prison but who subsequently accumulated twice that amount for offences committed during the course of his sentence.

In such an environment there was a daily expectation of violence. The history of the last thirty years at Peterhead has been a realization of that expectation.

An important feature of the debate in many prison systems about the management of prisoners who present the greatest threat to the safety of the public or to good order in prisons has been whether they should be concentrated in one location or dispersed across several. In 1966 Earl Mountbatten was appointed by the government to carry out an inquiry into prison security following an embarrassing series of escapes from English prisons. In his report[4] he recommended that those prisoners who required to be held in conditions of the greatest security should be held in one supersecure prison. This recommendation was not acceptable and two years later another committee[5] came up with the acceptable recommendation that these prisoners should be dispersed around a number of English prisons. This resulted in the dispersal system which is still in operation today.

The issue of concentration or dispersal did not arise at the time in Scotland because Peterhead was regarded as the only maximum security prison. But even the end of the line needed a fall-back position. In 1966 it was decided to convert part of the small local prison in Inverness, some 100 miles to the west of Peterhead, into a unit to hold those prisoners whose behaviour was such that both Peterhead and they needed a break from each other. The regime in the Inverness Unit for the five or six prisoners who were held there was officially described as spartan. Prisoners had virtually no facilities and were kept in their cells for most of the time. Despite this there was, from the time it opened, continuing disruption. The worst incident occurred in December 1972 when there was a major riot in which several officers and prisoners were seriously injured. The unit was closed two months later and during the succeeding six months ten out of the forty-three officers who worked in Inverness Prison resigned from the service.

During the 1970s the Inverness Unit became the symbolic focus in Scotland, both inside and outside the prison service, for the debate about how disruptive prisoners should be treated. The five cells in the unit were subdivided by installing a grille which separated the prisoner in each one from the staff. This arrangement inevitably led to the cells becoming known as 'the cages'.

The unit was reopened in 1978 and remained in virtually constant use until 1990. In 1984 the European Commission on Human Rights rejected a complaint by a prisoner that his period of detention in the unit constituted a breach of Article 3 of the European Convention on Human Rights. Whether or not the regime in the unit could be defined as 'torture or inhuman or degrading treatment or punishment', the message of the Inverness Unit for prisoners was quite clear. Violence would be met with repression, nonconformity would be met with coercion.

The existence of the Inverness Unit did not reduce the disruption at Peterhead. There were major incidents in 1975, 1977, 1978, 1979, 1982, 1984, 1985 and 1986. The riot and hostage-taking in the autumn of 1987 and its aftermath has already been referred to. In May 1988 after a trial held at a specially convened sitting of the High Court in Peterhead four prisoners received additional prison sentences totalling twenty-seven years for their parts in that incident. The following week I took up post as governor of Peterhead Prison.

THE GOVERNOR'S TALE

The atmosphere in Peterhead Prison in May 1988 was quite different from that in any other prison I had known. Prisons are never places of love and companionship. The reality is much too complex for that. But there is normally a sensation, at least at a superficial level, of mutual tolerance and an absence of overt aggression. Within the parameters required by security and good order prisoners and staff go about their daily business quietly and without confrontation. This was not the case at Peterhead.

The sixty high security prisoners were held in four separate groups; two of them on the lower landings of large halls which were otherwise empty, another group in a purpose-built unit with ten places and the fourth in what had originally been the punishment cells. The location of this last group summed up the extent to which management had been bled dry of constructive planning by the persistent daily battle with prisoners who refused to conform in any way with the restrictive regime.

The punishment unit consisted of sixteen cells on two storeys with no communal facilities for association. The cells were stripped of all furniture; only a raised concrete plinth on which the prisoner spread his bedding at night broke the symmetry of the rectangular box. In earlier years prisoners had regularly broken the strengthened glass in the cell windows and used the broken glass as a weapon with which to attack staff. Management's response had been to replace the glass by steel plates with drilled holes which allowed a minimum of ventilation and daylight. These cells were intended to be used only for short periods by prisoners who were being punished for breaches of discipline. Most of the prisoners who were there in May 1988 had been in these conditions for several months, if not years.

A newcomer to this environment was aware of the tension as soon as he crossed the threshold of the prison. It became more palpable with every step one took into the prison. Some of the prisoners were held in a block which overlooked the main entrance. Everyone who entered or left was under their surveillance and likely to be subjected to verbal abuse. Staff walked about with an unnatural quietness so as not to attract the attention of the prisoners.

The prisoners were all held under the provision of Prison Rule 36, that is, they were not allowed to have any contact with each other. They came out of their cells twice a day to perform their ablutions; once to take an hour's exercise if the weather permitted and from time to time if they asked to see a governor or another senior member of staff. Apart from infrequent visits from family or friends they spent the rest of each day locked in their spartan cells.

When they came out of their cells they were faced by at least three members of staff dressed in what was euphemistically described as protective clothing. This consisted of riot helmets, boiler suits and body armour. If the prisoner was thought to be in a particularly dangerous mood staff might also carry Perspex shields and wear protective padding on elbows and shins. A few months previously towering concrete pens had been built in which the prisoners were to take their daily exercise.

That was the regime which had been prescribed by management. The reality was slightly different. It is not possible for two groups of people who are thrown into such close proximity to be constantly formal with each other. Accommodations will be reached. What happened was that for periods at a time prisoners would outwardly conform to what was expected of them. Staff would then unofficially relax the regime. Prisoners would be allowed to spend time in each other's cell. Several would be allowed to exercise at once and, most commonly, two or three would be allowed to perform their ablutions at the same time. The 'archways', which were where the toilets and washbasins were situated, became the centre of what passed for community activity.

Every so often these informal accommodations would break down. Staff became complacent and reduced their surveillance. Prisoners would see their opportunity and would find a way to attack staff in a hopeless but dangerous manner with a razor blade melted into a toothbrush or even a ballpoint pen. Chamber pots full of human waste were frequent weapons. After every such incident the rules would be firmly applied for a period. The whole arrangement created a concertina effect with the regime being tightened, relaxed and then tightened again. There was no sense of any order or progression. No incentive for prisoners to conform; no confidence among staff to show any trust.

A new governor faced the challenge of trying to bring some decency, humanity and order into this environment. There were several audiences which had to be taken heed of. The first was the prisoners. They had been labelled as the most dangerous and subversive in the Scottish prison system but they were not an intrinsically homogeneous group. Some of them had been originally convicted of serious crimes of violence but there were men serving sentences quietly in other prisons who had been convicted of equally serious crimes so it was hard to argue that the danger presented by the men in Peterhead came solely from the nature of the crime which they had committed. Some of the prisoners had been involved directly in the serious incidents which had taken place over the preceding two or three years in this and other Scottish prisons. A number of them had received hefty additional sentences for taking hostages in these riots. Others were regarded as leaders among the prison population, men who had influence either through their force of personality or because of the connections which they had. Some people in authority in the Scottish prison system in the late 1980s took the view that a small number of prisoners, perhaps with external support, were coordinating the disturbances which were springing up in several prisons. If these people were taken out of the general population their ability to subvert good order would be critically diminished. Finally, one or two prisoners were there by unhappy coincidence. They had been in Peterhead when the decision to change the profile of the population had been made and they found themselves lumped in with the other groups.

The one factor which was a powerful bonding force for all prisoners was their hatred of being in Peterhead. For them it was a symbol on which to focus all their frustration and anger about being in prison. It symbolized the repressive nature of imprisonment, both physically and emotionally. The regime had no positive features, nor did it offer any hope for the future. Young men in their early twenties who had started with a life sentence and had ten or twelve years added because of the crimes they had committed while in prison had little reason for hope. And hopelessness led to dangerousness. Their hatred was expressed in a daily violence which was all the more tragic because in the end it was bound to be subjugated. Most of the men had been brought up in an environment in which might was right. This had been the case at home, in the school yard, in their dealings with each other and later with all other forms of authority. They expected violence to be met with violence. They understood that in prison the staff 'gang' was stronger than their 'gang'. They were not cowed by physical intimidation and saw it as legitimate to attempt to subvert official repression in every possible manner.

The second audience of which the new governor had to be aware was the staff. Many of them had spent the majority of their service at Peterhead. Almost as much as the prisoners, they felt themselves standing apart from their colleagues in other prisons. Peterhead was the end of the penal line. If prisoners refused to conform in other prisons the last option was to transfer them to Peterhead. In that respect it might be argued that Peterhead allowed other prisons to function. Yet there was an underlying feeling among staff elsewhere that Peterhead was something to be ashamed of, that it represented the unacceptable face of the prison service. This embarrassment was also attached to the staff of Peterhead, who were carrying out a task which no one else wished to admit existed and who were sullied in the process.

All of this ambivalence placed a great strain on the staff at Peterhead. They knew that they were carrying out a role for which they could expect little thanks or understanding. There was virtually no job satisfaction in going into the prison each day to don riot gear for an eight-hour shift during which they knew they would be subjected to considerable verbal abuse and might well be physically attacked. There was also an articulate body of opinion which argued that the only solution for Peterhead was that it should be closed.

Many of the uncertainties felt by staff in May 1988 were personalized on the incoming governor. He replaced a man who had been born in the shadow of the prison, who had grown up with many of the officers and who had been governor for over six years. There were fears that the new governor would not understand the need for firm management and would introduce a regime which would put staff at risk. An alternative scenario was that he had come with a secret instruction to ensure that the prison was run down with a view to closure.

The third audience to be aware of was a mixed bag of interested parties external to Peterhead. Prisons had been brought to the attention of Scottish politicians and public as never before because of the riots and disturbances which had taken place in the middle and late 1980s. It is a truism to say that there are no votes in prisons but votes can be lost because of what happens in prisons. Steps had to be taken to ensure that the front pages of daily newspapers were no longer full of prison disturbances. This consideration loomed large in the decision to hold those prisoners who were considered to be the most disruptive in Peterhead. Whatever was to be attempted in the prison, further disturbances which might result in bad publicity were to be avoided at all costs.

There was also considerable ambivalence about the future of Peterhead. It was an expensive prison in revenue terms relative to the number of prisoners which it held. Its staffing ratio was the highest in the country. There was general acceptance that the conditions in which prisoners were held fell far short of any acceptable norm. Yet no one in a position of authority was very clear about how to break out of the vicious circle.

RESTORING A DEGREE OF SANITY

If Peterhead was to break out of its spiral of violence someone had consciously to take the first step, had to begin to show a degree of trust which would allow others to respond in a human way. Despite the continuing indiscipline by the prisoners it was quite clear that power lay with the staff and it was they who would have to make the first move. In order to encourage them to do so without feeling that they were putting themselves at greater physical danger it was essential to bring a sense of structure to the way prisoners were treated. This meant bringing principle and practice closer together.

The key to dealing with any group of human beings is to see them as individuals. It has been a common error to view prisoners as a homogeneous group with a set of common values. The reality is that the only thing which most people who are in prison share with each other is the fact that they are in prison. The prisoners in Peterhead were further bound together in that they had been labelled as the most disruptive in the system and felt that they had to justify that description. Solidarity was their best protection against the environment in which they found themselves. It was important that they should be given some sense of their own worth and an expectation that through their behaviour they could regain some control over the circumstances in which they were placed.

There were three main strands to the new initiative. The first was to find a way out of Peterhead for a small but continuing number of prisoners. Return to a prison in 'the central belt' was the overriding ambition of all prisoners. If this prospect could be held out prisoners would have a reason to conform to legitimate rules and regulations. The greatest hurdle in this respect was to convince the governors of other long-term prisons that men who had been in Peterhead would not invariably be a disruptive influence on other prisoners. Prisoners had to be carefully selected and well briefed on the pressures which they would be likely to face in other prisons. In return it was agreed that if an individual prisoner in another prison began to present too many management problems the option of transfer to Peterhead would be available. This meant that Peterhead ceased to be a stagnant pool.

There was a need for a system of internal progression within Peterhead so that prisoners had practical incentives for observing the requirements of good order. The 'Rule 36' regime in which prisoners were dealt with one by one was reserved for those who had most recently arrived or who were most actively disruptive. A second group was allowed to mix in groups of three or four for most of each day. A third group of ten or so was allowed to move about freely within their unit.

Staff were encouraged to treat prisoners as individuals and not to base treatment of a group on the reaction of one individual. The regime in each group was kept under regular review but it was not relaxed or restricted as the prisoners within it behaved or mis-behaved. According to how an individual behaved he progressed or regressed to another group. There was the incentive for all of eventual transfer to another prison.

The final thread of the initiative was to move quite quickly towards closure of the punishment cells as a long-stay unit. They were quite inappropriate for other than very short-term stays and carried a great symbolism for both staff and prisoners. In the first five months of 1988 there were 98 assaults on staff in Peterhead and 95 per cent of these occurred in the punishment cells. The madness which was the punishment block in Peterhead has been described from a prisoner's perspective by John Steele in his book, *The Bird That Never Flew.* [6] He recounts a catalogue of violence and inhuman behaviour; of digging hopelessly from one cell to another; of having the window of his cell covered with sheet metal; of using his own faeces as a weapon against staff.

The principle of what was to be attempted was simple enough. Its application was much more difficult. Prisoners had to be convinced of the benefit of what was being proposed. Staff had to be reassured that the developments, far from putting their safety at risk, would improve security and good order in the prison. Once the plan had been agreed it was a question of keeping one's nerve. There were many uncomfortable moments. The journal which I kept at the time gives a flavour of one such:

12 February 1989: Mayhem in E Hall! At 4.30 p.m. a prisoner throws the video through the television set. When the Principal Officer steps in to lock him up he goes berserk and attacks staff. Others join in and for a few moments there is absolute bedlam, a battle royal with snooker balls and cues being used by the prisoners as the main weapons. Order is restored when staff reinforcements arrive. Five prisoners are involved and four take no part. It does not seem to have been premeditated, nor does there seem to have been any precipitating factor. I am left with the conclusion that the initial outburst may have been a reaction from a prisoner who had been locked up for a long time and who cannot handle even relative freedom of movement. Seven staff have been assaulted and three are taken to Aberdeen Royal Infirmary. One has eight stitches in a head wound.

13 February: An early morning meeting with the Scottish Prison Officers Association Local Committee. I expect a demand from them for a complete lock-up of the prison but that is not forthcoming. Apart from

an initial, 'We did warn you, Governor', they take a positive approach and we discuss how to salvage the situation. I say that I intend to leave the four non-combatants in the hall and we agree that if the maximum number of prisoners is kept at six for the time being the regime should continue as before. It is heartening that staff realize, even immediately after an event such as this, that further restrictions are no way to proceed.

In March 1989 there was a further setback. The prisoners in the most restrictive regime had been moved to a refurbished area and staff had been convinced that they should remove the riot gear which they had previously worn. Six prisoners managed to prise bed legs off and broke sizeable holes in the cell walls leading into the halls. The prisoners had to be returned to the area from which they had come and staff returned to wearing the 'protective clothing'.

When I left Peterhead Prison in May 1990 we could point to significant improvements. The number of prisoners held under Prison Rule 36 conditions had been reduced from more than 50 to ten. The number of unpaid work hours owed to staff had been reduced from 6,000 to virtually nil. The daily level of staff sickness had been reduced from 44 to an average of 18 and the number of assaults on staff in the first four months of that year was 16 compared to 70 in the equivalent period two years before.

My major regret on leaving Peterhead was that I had not convinced staff in one remaining area that the prisoners would never settle down while they were confronted daily by officers wearing helmets and body armour. In December 1992 *The Guardian* newspaper published a feature describing how the ten remaining difficult prisoners in Peterhead are now held in G Hall, looked after by staff wearing full riot gear.[7] I could not remember a G Hall in the prison. Then I realized that the punishment cells had been brought back into use under a new name.

DIFFICULT CHOICES

One of the greatest challenges to penal policy makers is the need to control the most violent prisoners in the country while at the same time exercising creativity in trying to devise and then try, on an experimental basis, activities that will not contribute to further deterioration of these inmates – deterioration which can lead in turn to greater risks of serious injury to staff, other prisoners, and often to the community upon the inmate's eventual release.[8]

The above quotation is an extract from a report on the United States Penitentiary, Marion, Illinois, prepared by two eminent American prison commentators. Marion has become an international byword for one model of how to manage the most dangerous prisoners. The prison was opened in 1963 as a replacement for the former penitentiary at Alcatraz in San Francisco Bay. In 1973 a secure unit was built within the maximum security prison to accommodate prisoners who were considered to be particularly dangerous.

Until October 1983 it was the practice that all prisoners in the unit were cuffed with hands to the front of their bodies whenever they came out of their cells. On 22 October 1983 a prisoner who was being escorted through a cell corridor by two officers was able to collect a hand-made knife passed through the grilled front of a cell and stabbed one of the escorting officers to death. Unbelievably a similar murder was committed that same afternoon by another prisoner who was determined to outdo the first one. The second prisoner had committed three previous murders in Marion.

Since that incident all prisoners have their hands cuffed behind their backs when moving outwith their cells. Prisoners are confined to their cells 23 hours each day and have virtually no contact with each other or with staff. Despite a great deal of informed concern and several official investigations the Federal Bureau of Prisons has concluded that there is no alternative but to maintain a regime such as this for the prisoners whom they consider to be the most dangerous.

Several of the United States have similar prisons, which are known as 'supermax' facilities. One of the most extreme examples is at Pelican Bay State Prison in California. This prison was opened in 1989. It was designed to hold over 1000 of the 'worst troublemakers' in the Californian prison system in an intensely regimented and restricted regime.

Twenty-two and a half hours a day are spent in the cells. The 'free' hour and a half is spent in an 'exercise yard' which is essentially a small bare concrete room with a high ceiling. Handcuffed and in waist chains, prisoners are put under double escort when they go to the 'yard' and once there they are continually monitored by cameras while they exercise in solitude.

Each concrete cell contains a concrete stool, concrete bed, concrete writing table, and a toilet and sink made of heavy stainless steel. Nothing is allowed on the walls. The cells are lined with opaque materials so that prisoners cannot see out. Prisoners never walk freely, they never emerge from their cells without being handcuffed and in chains.[9]

There are two problems with this method of dealing with prisoners who refuse to accept the legitimate restrictions of security and good order in a prison. One is a matter of principle; the other a matter of good practice. Article 7 of the International Covenant on Civil and Political Rights provides that

> No one shall be subjected to torture or to cruel, inhuman or degrading treatment or punishment.

Article 10 of the same Covenant includes the following guiding principle:

> All persons deprived of their liberty shall be treated with humanity and respect for the inherent dignity of the human person.

It can be argued with justification that keeping prisoners in what amounts to permanent isolation, being dealt with on a regular basis by staff wearing riot gear or being required to wear chains whenever they come out of their cells amounts to a breach of one or both of these international norms. Administrative behaviour which is publicly criticized when it occurs in a totalitarian state is even less acceptable in a democratic society.

The good practice argument is simply that such treatment is counterproductive. It militates against good order. One cannot subjugate another person into good behaviour. Prisoners will respond to what they regard as institutional violence in a violent manner, even when their situation is quite hopeless. The consequence is that both sides, staff and prisoners, will adopt even more extreme positions.

Prisoners who present the most serious threat to good order have to be given a reason to conform to the normal requirements of prison life. Achieving this is a real test of the professionalism and humanity of a prison administration. Real power lies not with the prisoners but with the administrators. It is they who must be creative in providing positive incentives for good behaviour.

GOOD PRACTICE

There are examples across the world of pockets of good practice. If Marion and Peterhead represented unacceptable methods of dealing with prisoners who present serious problems for management, it is fair to point out that within the same prison systems there are two good examples of positive practice. The Federal Institution at Butner, North Carolina, was opened in 1976 and holds prisoners of all security categories, including a number who have presented severe problems for management during the course of their sentences. Some of these have come directly from the Special Handling Unit at Marion Penitentiary.

The prison is laid out in campus style, with prisoners located 30/40 to a living unit. Cells are opened at 6.00 each morning. During the day prisoners are allowed free movement within each block of two units. They make their own way to worksheds and to the various departments such as education, sports hall, and surgery, which are located round a central green. All prisoners are involved in some form of constructive daily activity. They carry their own cell keys. At 11.30 each night they are required to go to their rooms or to an adjacent television area.

The regime in the prison is based directly on that proposed by the eminent American criminologist, Norval Morris.[10] It aims to provide a secure and humane environment in which a prisoner, aware of his release date and with a graduated release plan, can focus attention on acquiring self-knowledge and control. Each prisoner spends an hour each week with a personal counsellor. At regular intervals he takes part in an evaluation of his progress and his needs.

Butner has been described as 'the jewel of the federal system'.[11] Its main achievement has been to help men to cope with their sentences and to encourage them to take part in the programmes which are available. The research evidence shows that the prisoners at Butner are less likely to assault each other or to become involved in breaches of discipline than a comparative group in other prisons.

The Special Unit in Barlinnie Prison, Glasgow, was opened in 1972. It was set up in recognition of the need to provide something other than a repressive response to the continuing cycle of violence into which some Scottish long-term prisoners were locked. The unit can hold up to eight prisoners. All will be serving long sentences and have usually been involved in some form of violence or serious incident during their time in prison. Prisoners with serious psychiatric or drug problems are not admitted to the unit.

The main community activities centre around a series of regular meetings. The most important of these is the formal weekly community meeting. Those present, both prisoners and staff, elect a chairman and a record is kept of the discussion which can range over any issue relevant to the community. There is no formal system of punishment within the unit. A serious breach of rules may result in a transfer from the unit. When internally agreed procedures are broken, the person concerned has to explain his actions to other members of the community. There is no structured programme of work but prisoners are encouraged to develop personal interests in art, sculpting, education, woodwork, physical training or hobbies.

One of the main features of the unit is that prisoners are allowed virtually unlimited visits. After an initial period these may be taken in the man's own cell, all of which have been fitted out at the prisoner's own expense as sitting rooms.

David Cooke, a psychologist who has worked at and carried out research in the unit for a number of years, has charted the reduction in violent behaviour among those prisoners who have spent some time in the unit.[12] He attributes this to a number of situational factors, such as relative autonomy in day-to-day matters and the support and ability to ventilate problems afforded by community meetings. Central to all of this is the positive relationship between staff and prisoners. Regular and extensive visits from families and friends also play an important part in the success of the unit. Cooke points to the importance of intrinsic change, such as the ability which men develop to express their feelings verbally rather than physically, the access which they have to a non-criminal network and the opportunity to develop creative talents.

END PIECE

An important measure of the professionalism of any prison service is the manner in which it cares for those prisoners who present a serious threat to security or to good order. In most prisons there is at least a veneer of forbearance and an acceptance that rules and regulations have to be observed. If, however, prisoners refuse, for whatever reason, to accept the reality of imprisonment, the stark fact of the coercive nature of imprisonment comes immediately to the surface.

When faced with prisoners who are continually obstructive or even destructive, the temptation which faces prison staff is to meet conflict with conflict, to respond to illegal violence with legalized violence. This is a response which will probably ensure short-term control but which in the long run will militate against good order.

One of the lessons of imprisonment is that only by treating people decently are they likely to respond in a decent manner. Whatever disruption prisoners may cause, it is important to remember that real power always lies in the hands of the authorities and it is they who must set standards. In his report on prison disturbances in England and Wales in 1990[13] Lord Justice Woolf took the trouble to quote from a letter which he had received from a prisoner:

> It is obvious if prisoners are treated like animals, sworn at, degraded and psychologically toyed with week after week, they in turn lose respect, not only for their tormentors, but for society at large (para. 14.3).

The negative lesson of prisons like Marion and Peterhead is that they are not places of good order and that control is achieved only through subjugation. The positive lesson of prisons such as Butner and the Barlinnie Special Unit is that if people, even those who are most difficult and disruptive, are treated in a humane and responsible manner they are more likely to respond in similar vein.

REFERENCES

1. Scottish Record Office, File HH/57/101.
2. Criminal Justice (Scotland) Act 1949, Section 16.
3. 'The Roof Comes Off' (1987), The Report of the Independent Committee of Inquiry into the Protests at Peterhead Prison, Gateway Exchange, Edinburgh.
4. Report of the Inquiry into Prison Escapes and Security (1966), HMSO, London, Cmnd 3175.
5. Report of the Advisory Council on the Penal System on the Regime for Long-term Prisoners in Conditions of Maximum Security (1968), HMSO, London.
6. Steele, J (1992), *The Bird That Never Flew*, Sinclair-Stevenson, London.
7. *The Guardian*, 9 December 1992.
8. Ward, D & Breed, A (1985), Report on the US Penitentiary, Marion, presented to the Committee on the Judiciary of the US House of Representatives, US Government Printing Office, Washington.
9. *The National Prison Project Journal*, Vol. 7, No 4, Fall 1992, Washington.
10. Morris, N (1974), *The Future of Imprisonment*, University Press, Chicago.
11. Smith, R (1984), 'Prison Health Care', British Medical Association, London.
12. Cooke, D J (1989), 'Containing Violent Prisoners: An Analysis of the Barlinnie Special Unit', British Journal of Criminology, Vol. 29, No 2, Spring 1989.
13. Report of an Inquiry into Prison Disturbances April 1990 (1991), HMSO, London, Cmnd 1456.

EIGHT

Coming out of Solitary

THE GOVERNOR'S TALE

On 7 July 1991 two high security remand prisoners who were accused of involvement in terrorist offences shot their way out of Brixton Prison. The subsequent public outcry almost cost the Home Secretary of the day his job.

The governor had been due to retire in October 1991 and I had already accepted an invitation to take command of the troubled South London prison after he had done so. Following the escape the Home Secretary appointed Judge Tumim, Her Majesty's Chief Inspector of Prisons, to carry out an investigation. He submitted his report to the Home Secretary at the beginning of August 1991. On Friday 2 August I was summoned to prison service head-quarters within the Home Office and told that I was to take command of Brixton Prison with immediate effect. At the same time my predecessor was told that he had to take immediate pre-retirement leave.

On Monday 5 August I was summoned to meet the Home Secretary, who was accompanied by the Minister of State with responsibility for prisons. The meeting was relatively brief. The Home Secretary said, 'Governor, I have only one thing to say to you. There must be no more escapes.' Later that day the Home Secretary announced the findings of the Chief Inspector's investigation. During the entire month between the escape and the publication of the Chief Inspector's report there had been continuing press speculation about the circumstances of the escape and the relative responsibility of those in authority. This intensified with the publication of the report.

Such was my introduction to Brixton Prison.

Brixton Prison was opened in 1819 as the Surrey House of Correction. With the exception of brief spells as an army detention centre and a women's prison, its main task over the last hundred years was to hold prisoners who were awaiting or who were on trial at any of the crown courts in Greater London. Staff were responsible for escorting prisoners to and from crown courts and for staffing the cells and dock areas of crown courts in Hertfordshire, Essex, Middlesex, Sussex, Surrey and London. The prison had the largest staff in the country, over 200 of whom worked in crown courts. The prison looked squarely towards servicing the courts. It concentrated on getting the right prisoner to the right court on the right day. It took pride in its ability to cope with the immediate problem. On any one day up to 200 prisoners would leave the prison during a ninety-minute period in the morning and a similar number would return each evening. In a word, the prison served the courts very well.

Within the prison a terrible price was paid for this efficiency. The establishment took a perverse pride in squeezing up to 1150 men into 730 cells. In many cases there would be three prisoners in a cell designed for one man. There were virtually no activities for the prisoners, who were locked up for twenty-three hours each day. There were no worksheds, no education unit and no sports field. A gymnasium had been built in the 1970s but it was outside the secure perimeter of the prison and could not be used by prisoners. Brixton was a large prison crowded into a very small area. It was no exaggeration to describe it as a human warehouse.

Since it held prisoners who were facing trial on all types of charges, including the most serious, it held up to sixty Category A prisoners; that is, those who required to be held in maximum security conditions. This was a greater number than was held in some purpose-built high security prisons. Brixton did not have the level of physical security which was usual for holding such prisoners. When he inspected the prison in 1990 the Chief Inspector of Prisons expressed concern at this. It was two of these prisoners who escaped in July 1991.

The prison also held up to 300 men who had been remanded in custody for some form of medical report, usually of a psychiatric nature. 230 of these men were held in F Wing. That number of individuals would fill a fair-sized psychiatric hospital. But F Wing was not a psychiatric hospital. It was a typical Victorian prison wing with four open galleries. The prisoner/patients spent twenty-three hours each day in standard cells, with an iron bed, a table, a chair and a chamber pot for company. Staff were grossly overworked and spent all day rushing about simply to ensure that prisoners received their statutory minimum entitlements in respect of food, water and exercise.

The last thing which these prisoners, many of whom were severely disturbed, needed was to be confined in these conditions. If a man was not unstable before admission to F Wing, he was likely soon to become so. Between 1989 and 1990 there were fourteen suicides in the prison, the majority of them in F Wing. Staff felt that above all they had to protect themselves from the further criticism which a coroner's inquest would bring. If a prisoner showed any sign that he might harm himself he would be placed in a 'strip cell'. As the name implied, this was a concrete cell stripped of all furniture. The prisoner himself was stripped of normal clothing. He wore a heavy duty smock which was allegedly tear-proof. He had a sleeping bag made of the same material which was placed on the concrete floor. The most disturbed men were held in these conditions. Almost all of these men were remand prisoners, yet to be found guilty of any offence.

I shall never forget the first day I walked into F Wing. Nothing in my twenty years in the prison service, not even the extremes of Peterhead, had prepared me for what I encountered. The walls were painted bottle green. Permanent semi-darkness meant that artificial lighting had to be kept on all day. The all-pervading smell was over-powering: a combination of urine, faeces and stale food. And the noise. An unrelenting cacophony of keening, wailing, shouting and banging, which went on even during the night. Each cell had a large flap in its door. These were usually open. A face, usually a black face, peered out from most of them, hungry for human contact.

Small wonder that Judge Tumim, Her Majesty's Chief Inspector of Prisons, in a report published in 1990,[1] had described the prison as 'a corrupting and depressing institution', strong words even for the usually frank Judge Tumim. In 1991 the European Committee for the Prevention of Torture[2] found that the 'pernicious combination of overcrowding, inadequate regime activities, lack of integral sanitation and poor hygiene' in Brixton and in some other English prisons amounted to 'inhuman and degrading treatment'.

RESTORING A SENSE OF DIGNITY

In August 1991 Brixton was a prison on its knees. For many years it had survived because of staff pride in their ability to do the impossible. 'The daily miracle' had been achieved at a great price, but it had been achieved. The price was paid by prisoners who were locked up for twenty-three hours each day in inhuman conditions without any prospect of constructive activity. It was paid by their families who came to visit them in a cramped and unattractive visiting room. And it was paid by staff who had to work in unhygienic conditions, which at times were unsafe. Before 1987 staff had regularly worked long hours of overtime with the consolation that they were paid for the extra hours they worked. Since 1987 they had continued to work additional hours, but without extra payment. Instead they were credited with excess hours and in theory were allowed to take them off at a later date. In 1991 management owed staff 30,000 hours' time off for additional hours which had been worked.

Suddenly, following the escape of 7 July 1991, the invulnerability of the machine was in question. Perhaps Brixton could not cope after all. The nightmare continued into the winter of 1991. A disciplinary inquiry was set up by the Home Office into the circumstances of the escape. It recommended that three officers should be disciplined and concluded that had the former governor not retired he too would have faced disciplinary proceedings. The number of prisoners rose significantly and the closure of one wing for refurbishment, which was to mark the beginning of the new Brixton, had to be delayed. A coroner's inquiry found that the death of a prisoner earlier in the year had been due to 'lack of care'. 1991 ended with further criticism of Brixton in the report by the European Committee for the Prevention of Torture. Suddenly Brixton was everyone's whipping boy.

There is a particular challenge in taking over an organization which has been rocked to its foundations. If it has reached its nadir there is a great opportunity, particularly if it has an innate strength and confidence, to rebuild it within a new and more dynamic context. Brixton had that latent capability.

As a prison Brixton was a very complex institution. It had the population of a large prison but was contained in a very small area. It had few internal facilities. It had the highest daily throughput of prisoners in the country. At the same time it held sixty prisoners in the highest security category. It had the seemingly intractable problem of a large number of mentally disturbed prisoners. It had a high suicide rate. Many prisons had one or two of these problems. None had all of them under one roof.

The problem of Brixton as an institution was recognized by many people who had some indirect responsibility either for the kind of people who were sent there or for the conditions in which they were held. But no one was sure how to unravel the Gordian knot. There was a conspiracy of silence, a collusion of refusal to admit that something needed to be done. Brixton was a terrible place. There were plenty of people willing to admit that – and to place the shame on Brixton, without recognizing that the shame had to be shared by all who worked within the criminal justice system and beyond.

One of the most obvious signs of this conspiracy of silence was the secrecy which surrounded Brixton. For ten years virtually no press or media had been allowed inside the prison. There were relatively few visitors from outside the prison service or indeed from inside the service. It was as though people feared contamination by association. There were two consequences of this isolation. The public, through the media, were led to believe that something terrible was going on at Brixton. Secondly, the staff, who in reality were doing their best in impossible circumstances, had the feeling that they must have something, although they did not know what, to be ashamed of.

ENCOURAGING PUBLIC SCRUTINY

Many people have a great sense of ambivalence about prisons and this was particularly true in the case of Brixton. They feel relief and sometimes satisfaction when they hear of people who have committed serious crimes being sent to prison. At the same time there is often unease at the notion that people, many of them not yet guilty of any offence, are locked up in conditions which border on the inhumane. This ambivalence is sometimes expressed in an odd combination of a desire to know what goes on behind the high walls of a prison coupled with a refusal to recognize that prisons are the way they are because society wants them that way. If prisons are terrible places, that must be the fault of the people who run them.

One of the first initiatives at Brixton was to let the public, through the media, have a glimpse of what life inside was like. In December 1991 a facility visit was offered to the press. They came in their numbers. Staff were briefed in advance why this was happening. They were told that they should show the press everything and should speak to them about how they went about their daily task of caring for the prisoners. Prisoners were also told that they could speak to the journalists if they so wished. This was undoubtedly a high risk strategy. There was a danger that staff would be totally critical of all that was being done or that they would appear to be uncaring in their attitude towards prisoners. There was the possibility that prisoners would react against the presence of the cameras or would make all sorts of allegations about their treatment.

In the event, the visit achieved all that was intended. The journalists and cameramen spent half a day in the prison and were allowed to see the reality of life in an old, overcrowded, under-resourced local prison. Staff explained the manner in which they tried to carry out their duties in a humane way. Prisoners said what a terrible place Brixton was but distinguished that from the way they were treated by staff. The copy in the newspapers the following day reflected this reality. The articles documented the problems of overcrowding, of the mentally ill and of the lack of facilities. But they also showed that staff were making the best of a bad job and that they showed concern in the way they dealt with prisoners. A start had been made in the task of rehabilitating Brixton.

It had required some effort to convince people in the Home Office Press Branch that there was more to be gained than to be lost by opening Brixton to the press in this way. Given the continuing media interest in the aftermath of the escape and its attendant publicity their caution was to some extent understandable. Arguably they should themselves have been working out a media strategy for Brixton.

The next step was to harness the power of television. On the basis that a picture is worth a thousand words, it was important to give a much wider audience an impression of life in Brixton. In January 1992 a Channel 4 television news team was invited to spend two days in the prison to prepare a ten-minute piece for their evening news programme on the changes which were taking place at Brixton. The agenda was as before and again the outcome of the operation was successful.

After that it was time to become more focused in the use of the media. It had been clear from an early stage that the most pressing problem at Brixton was the management of those prisoners who were mentally disordered or disoriented. The strongest public criticism of Brixton was reserved for its treatment of these men and for the fact that so many of them had died in custody. But the staff of Brixton did not go out to sweep these men off the street. They were sent to prison by properly constituted courts of law. Many of them remained there because places could not be found for them in psychiatric hospitals. It was important that the issues should be opened up for public debate.

Several of the major television documentary companies expressed an interest in coming into Brixton. Agreement was reached with BBC's 'Public Eye' that they should make a programme. Their team spent two weeks in the prison, going to all parts, speaking to people and listening. They spent a further two weeks filming. The programme went out in two parts in successive weeks in February 1992. The first part concentrated on the plight of the mentally disordered offenders. It showed the terrible conditions in which they were kept but it also showed that staff were as caring as was possible in impossible circumstances. The root of the problem lay not in Brixton but in a system which sent men such as these to prison.

The reaction to the programme, both immediately and in the longer term, was as we had hoped. Shortly after transmission a senior official of the Department of Health asked to visit the prison. There was discussion about setting up a project to divert disordered offenders from the prison. Contact with local psychiatric hospitals and with other community provision improved noticeably. Of equal importance was the fact that staff now felt that their work was better understood. They had a greater confidence as they went about their duties caring as best they could for these unfortunate men.

THE MENTALLY DISTURBED OFFENDER

Over the past decade and more there has been increasing concern at the number of mentally disordered people who are finding their way into the criminal justice system. There are many reasons why this has happened and little is to be gained by trying to apportion blame for the way we treat this group of men and women. It is important for us to recognize that the problem exists and that we should reach a solution which treats such people with the care and supervision which they deserve, while also recognizing the need to protect society.

We have had a tradition in the United Kingdom, dating from Victorian times, of locking up too many people in institutions of one sort or another. We like tidiness in our society and in this respect out of sight is out of mind. In addition, the restrictions which were applied in many of these institutions were more severe than was necessary. It was a recognition of this fact which led some twenty or so years ago to a progressive unlocking of the wards of our large psychiatric hospitals. Many of the men and women in these hospitals did not require to be cared for in such secure conditions. Indeed, their recovery was being made more difficult by the fact that they were allowed to have no contact with the rest of society. It was right and proper that these hospitals should be made much more accessible and that patients should have much more freedom of movement. Unfortunately there was a minority of patients who could not cope with this reduction in security.

Over the years, as the number of locked wards in local psychiatric hospitals reduced, there was more likelihood that doctors would assess this minority as being unsuitable for hospital treatment. For many of them the alternative when they committed a series of minor but persistent offences was that they would end up in prison. This possibility increased as the number of model lodging houses in major cities was reduced. Even the disappearance of brickworks, where these casualties of our society could keep themselves warm at night, had an effect on the number who were sucked into the criminal justice system.

It has to be remembered that many of the men and women who are locked up in our prisons are not major criminals who pose a threat to the rest of us as we go about our lawful business. Instead, they are inadequate men and women who find it very difficult to survive.

There have been several studies in recent years which have confirmed the number of prisoners who have some kind of mental disorder. In 1991 the Home Office published the results of a study into the psychiatric state of convicted prisoners. [3] This study found that 37 per cent of male prisoners and 56 per cent of female prisoners serving sentences of six months or more may have a medically identifiable disorder. 3 per cent of them were diagnosed as being in need of urgent transfer to hospital.

The study, which was carried out by a team led by Professor John Gunn of the Institute of Psychiatry, painted a disturbing picture of the treatment of some of these disturbed people:

> In some prison hospitals, it is possible to see an acutely psychotic patient locked in a cell for the whole day. He may be clad only in a canvas shift with no possessions or furniture other than a mattress, possibly soaked in urine or soiled with faeces. Compulsory treatment can only be given in an emergency. Patients kept in such conditions in the health service would be the cause of public outcry and an enquiry. The situation is no more defensible when it occurs in prison.

In 1991 Brixton Prison held a higher number of mentally disordered prisoners than any other prison in the United Kingdom. A disturbing reason for this was that the main task of Brixton at that time was to hold prisoners who were awaiting trial at courts across metropolitan London. Almost all of the mentally disordered prisoners at Brixton were to be found among the remand prisoners. This fact was examined in a study carried out in 1991 by a team from the Institute of Criminology at Cambridge University. [4] The team examined the situation of remand prisoners in Brixton Prison, in Risley Remand Centre and in Holloway Women's Prison. It contrasted the low level of remands to hospital for psychiatric assessment, which was about 300 each year in England and Wales, with the volume of psychiatric reports by prison doctors on remanded prisoners, which was approximately twenty times greater.

The study found that people remanded for psychiatric reports were more likely to have been charged with public order offences, such as criminal damage, threatening behaviour, possession of an offensive weapon or vagrancy, than with serious offences of violence. Mentally disordered people were more likely to be remanded in custody because of their need for social and psychiatric help than because of the nature of their offences. Ironically, such men and women were more likely to spend longer in prison on remand than those who did not require a medical report. The situation was even worse once a person had been assessed as requiring hospital care. At Brixton the team found that:

> The average delay between someone being accepted for a bed by an NHS doctor and that person's admission to hospital was between 5 and 6 weeks. It is impossible to imagine a situation in the community in which a consultant, having carried out a domiciliary visit and having agreed that the person concerned needed to be detained in hospital, would then arrange for admission in 6 weeks' time.

In December 1990 the government established a steering group under the chairmanship of Dr John Reed to review the health and social services for mentally disordered offenders. The group completed its work in 1992.[5] The findings of the review paint a sorry picture. Its conclusions are summed up in the following comment:

> The Government's long-standing policy has been that mentally disordered offenders needing care and treatment should receive it from the health and personal social services rather than in custodial care. However, we recognize that practice all too often falls a long way short of what is desirable.

In many respects it was providential that attempts to deal with the problem of mentally disordered offenders held in Brixton Prison got underway just when official awareness of the problem was being heightened. This had led to increased efforts to divert such people from the criminal justice system into the health service at the point of arrest or at least at the point of court appearance. This had led to an increased willingness within the health service to deal with the issue. Initiatives at Brixton to transfer to hospital mentally disordered men who had reached the prison received a generally positive response from psychiatrists and others in the health service.

The number of mentally disordered men held in Brixton fell dramatically. The final breakthrough came at the beginning of 1993 when the last of the disturbed prisoners was removed from the infamous F Wing, which had been known to the prisoners as Fraggle Rock. From then on all such prisoners were held in one of five health care wards, where they received proper medical supervision.

RACE AND IMPRISONMENT

Discrimination on racial grounds does not necessarily occur when somebody is consciously motivated by racial prejudice. It may also take the form of indirect discrimination. Members of ethnic minorities may receive different treatment from others, when the fact that they possess different characteristics, social or otherwise, influences the decisions which are being made about them during the criminal justice process.[6]

One of the aspects of Brixton Prison which strikes a visitor immediately is that such a large proportion of the prisoners are black, so many that they almost cease to be a minority. The percentage is between 35 and 40. Even taking account of the ethnic mix of the population in London as a whole this figure requires some explanation.

Just under 5 per cent of the population of England and Wales belong to an ethnic minority.[7] The Home Office survey on race in the criminal justice system which is referred to at the head of this section reported that unemployment among ethnic minorities, particularly young males, is higher than among whites. Ethnic minorities are more likely than whites to live in high crime areas. They are also more likely to be victims of crime. Afro-Caribbeans are more likely than any other racial group to be stopped by the police. They are also more likely to be remanded in custody if charged with an offence. A study carried out in 1989 showed that, on the basis of the raw data, in the West Midlands of England black males had a 17 per cent greater chance of receiving a custodial sentence than whites. 17 per cent of the prison population in England and Wales described themselves in a 1991 survey as belonging to an ethnic minority. [9]

A discussion about why so many black people are sent to prison is the subject for another book. The treatment of these prisoners is a matter of great concern for those who work in the prison system. About one per cent of prison staff in England and Wales are black. It is difficult to be precise about this figure since some staff have been reluctant to respond to a request for information about their racial origin. It has been suggested that one reason for the under-representation of ethnic minorities among prison staff is the system which existed until recently of recruitment at a national level. It has been suggested that those who applied to join the prison service were more likely to come from parts of the country where there is a low ethnic minority population. One must also recognize that many black members of our community have grave reservations about working in what they fear may be a racist environment. A great deal of work has been done but much remains to be done to convince members of ethnic minorities that we want them and need them to work in the prison service.

Since 1993 recruitment of staff to work in prisons has been carried out at individual establishments. It may be that one consequence of this will be a more representative recruitment to prisons in communities where there is a large black population. Certainly the proportion of 5 per cent of staff at Brixton Prison who are black is far lower than that in the local population. The need for improvement in this area has been underlined by HM Chief Inspector of Prisons: [10]

> We believe that many racial difficulties in prisons would
> be further resolved by the recruitment of more staff
> from ethnic minorities.

The first circular instruction on race relations was issued by the prison service in 1981. Since then there has been a steady stream of central initiatives designed to encourage better race relations in the prison system. There is a national Race Relations Group which acts as a forum in which experience and expertise can be pooled and successful initiatives can be shared. Each prison has a race relations liaison officer who works to a race relations management team. Each establishment's annual contract makes specific reference to the implementation of race relations policies.

The reality of race relations in a prison is that there has to be constant vigilance on matters of diet and of access to religious ministration. In Brixton about 10 per cent of prisoners are Muslim. Regular monitoring takes place of the proportion of black prisoners who have access to education or who are given employment in the prison, as well as the proportion who are charged with breaches of discipline. Race relations can also have a positive aspect. The period of imprisonment can be used to open all prisoners to cultural interests which they might not otherwise experience.

Despite these efforts, the achievements in the field of race relations in many prisons leaves much to be desired. The Woolf Report[11] had this to say on the subject:

> The conclusion which the Inquiry draws from the evidence which is available is that, despite the Prison Service's good intentions, there is still a need for further progress if a satisfactory position with regards to race relations is to be achieved in prisons.

EXTRAJUDICIAL DEATHS

This chilling phrase is used to refer to deaths which occur in prison other than those authorized by a court, that is to say, legal executions. In some countries these deaths may be caused by ill-treatment of a prisoner by staff or by fellow prisoners. Mercifully this type of death in the prisons of the United Kingdom occurs rarely. Yet there is a disturbing number of extrajudicial deaths in our prisons each year. In 1991 71 prisoners died, including a number who were transferred to outside hospitals before death.[12] Of these, 17 died from natural causes, four died from 'non-natural causes' and in six cases inquest verdicts were awaited at the time of the report. 43 deaths were self-inflicted, 30 of these were defined formally as suicides.

The annual toll of self-inflicted deaths in prisons in England and Wales has been a cause for public concern for a number of years.

In 1990 the Home Secretary asked Judge Stephen Tumim, HM Chief Inspector of Prisons, to investigate the level of suicide and self-harm in prisons and to recommend whether arrangements for the prevention of suicide, particularly among mentally disturbed prisoners, needed to be changed. Tumim found that most self-inflicted deaths took place among the remand population. 33 per cent of the prisoners who took their own lives had a history of previous psychiatric contact and 25 per cent of them had at some previous point been patients in psychiatric hospitals. His wide-ranging report[13] included 123 recommendations. The most important ones were that the prevention of suicide should not be regarded solely as a medical matter and that every element of prison life had a possible bearing on how people responded to the fact of imprisonment.

Reference has already been made to the fact that between 1989 and 1990 14 prisoners in Brixton died at their own hand. At the inquest on a suicide which occurred in May 1991 the coroner's inquest uncovered a sorry tale of a disoriented young man who slipped further and further into a depressive state because of a series of events connected with his personal circumstances, his pending trial and his imprisonment. The relentless machine which was Brixton at that time failed to pick up the distress which the young man was experiencing and he eventually took his own life. The conclusion of the inquest was that he had committed suicide due to a lack of care. This was a damning indictment of the prison. It was also a damning indictment of a society which required young men to be locked up in such conditions.

The dramatic reduction in the number of mentally disturbed men held in Brixton which has been described above meant that staff were able to spot those who were most likely to attempt to injure themselves and to give them proper support. The practice of keeping such prisoners in isolated cells without any personal comfort or possession was stopped. Instead they were usually held in small wards where they could mix with other prisoners and where staff had time to listen to them.

If a prisoner harmed himself, however superficially, a meeting would immediately be held of everyone who had any direct interest in him. This would include the landing officer, the health care officer, the medical officer, the probation officer and others such as the chaplain. Crucially, whenever possible the man himself was invited to attend and to discuss what had led him to his despairing action.

As in other prisons, there was a Suicide Awareness Group which met regularly to discuss individual cases, and a strategy for ensuring that the possibility of self-harm was kept to a minimum. Local Samaritan groups were involved as were other prisoners.

Prison is an abnormal environment which can never be entirely stress-free. Even when all precautions have been taken one is left with the possibility that a person who is determined to take his own life may succeed in doing so. In December 1992 and in February 1993 two young men hanged themselves in Brixton Prison. In both cases they were being held in ordinary cells and staff had no reason to believe that they were particularly vulnerable. In one case the inquest jury returned an open verdict. In the other the verdict was that the young man had killed himself. At both inquests the coroner commended the actions of staff who had tried to save the young men's lives.

VULNERABLE PRISONERS

Prisons should be safe places for those who live there and for those who work there. People who are deprived of their liberty should not have the additional punishment of fearing for their personal safety while they are in prison. In many countries throughout the world prisons are not safe places. I remember being struck during a visit to a federal prison in the United States some years ago when the warden said, 'We have learned that if the number of murders of prisoners does not go above eleven in a year we are not likely to be criticized.' The Americas Watch report on Prison conditions in Brazil[14] paints a frightening picture of the anarchy in that country's prisons:

> Perhaps the most distinctive and tragic aspect of Brazilian prisons is the use of inmate murder as a protest against prison conditions.

Murders of this sort are the result of random or organized violence which happens to take place in a prison setting. Such incidents are relatively rare in the United Kingdom. There is another expression of prisoner on prisoner violence which does have a peculiarly British aspect.

As a group, prisoners are surprisingly judgemental. They have a moralistic hierarchy which places major criminals, such as armed robbers, at the top of a pecking order, coming down through those who have committed personal violence and property offenders. At the bottom of this hierarchy are those who have been convicted of sexual offences. Within this group, those who have offended against the most vulnerable, such as old people or the young, are most despised.

This hierarchy has always existed. What has changed in recent years is the physical violence which some prisoners are prepared to inflict on other prisoners, particularly those convicted of offences of a sexual nature. It is difficult to be precise about why this should have happened in British prisons in a fashion which has not occurred in other countries. It may be partly ascribed to the publicity given to such cases in the tabloid press which almost encourages other prisoners to place themselves in the role of vigilantes on behalf of society. Pleas in mitigation by defence counsel that accused persons will be subject to physical assault if they are sent to prison certainly do not discourage prisoners from such violence.

Whatever the reason it has become increasingly necessary in recent years to segregate prisoners accused or convicted of sexual offences from other prisoners. In Brixton a small unit was set up in 1992 to hold prisoners who were subject to threat from other prisoners. One of the most disturbing features of this arrangement is that many of the prisoners held in this unit are on remand, not yet convicted of any offence. It is a sad reflection of the hypocrisy of our society that prisoners should place themselves in positions of judgement over their fellows.

In some prisons the fact that these prisoners require to be segregated for their own safety has been taken as an opportunity to set up courses which attempt to oblige them to confront the terrible offences which they have committed. It is as yet too early to evaluate the success of these courses. There is a strong argument on grounds of public safety for embarking on such a course of action. The prison service has become more aware in recent years of its obligation to help prisoners to face up to the offences which they have committed. The most difficult group to deal with are probably those who have been convicted of sexual offences. It is ironic that the trigger for starting with them was the fact that they became an identifiable group because they had to be protected from other prisoners.

FAMILY AND COMMUNITY LINKS

One of the challenges facing any prison administrator is to minimize the damage which prison does to a person. This is important for the personal development of the individual concerned. It is also important in the interests of society. People who come out with strong links to family or friends and a sense that they have something to contribute to their community are less likely to commit further crime than those who leave prison with a sense of bitterness and alienation from the community to which they have returned.

Many prisons are built in isolated locations which underline the notion of prison as a place of exile. It is extremely difficult to foster a real sense of community when the majority of prisoners are several hundred miles away from their homes. This should not be a problem in prisons which are situated in our great cities. There the problems are of a different dimension.

The majority of prisoners in Brixton are awaiting committal or trial. According to prison rules they are entitled to a daily visit lasting fifteen minutes. Until recently Brixton had a turnover of about 30,000 prisoners each year. Simply ensuring that the majority of them received their legal visit entitlement was a major exercise. Staff can remember not so long ago when the visit room consisted of fifteen enclosed glass cubicles. Visitors would queue in the street outside the prison. Prisoners would form a similar queue inside the prison. The two queues, like cogs in a massive machine, would move on at fifteen-minute intervals. Prisoners received their daily entitlement but there was little hope of any real communication with the visitors. At the end of each day's visiting someone had the task of going down the row of cubicles cleaning the glass on either side of fingermarks and impressions of lips where people had engaged in a forlorn attempt to make contact.

Visiting arrangements in Brixton have improved considerably since those days. Prisoners now sit across an open table from their visitors. Remand prisoners can choose to aggregate visits into longer periods. The reduction in the number of men in the prison has meant that visits can generally last longer than the statutory minimum period. It remains very difficult in this environment to have other than a superficial discussion with one's visitors. There is no real privacy and one is always conscious of the proximity of others.

Subject to the legitimate demands of security and the need to protect the public, there is an obligation on any prison system to encourage prisoners to maintain family links. If the prisoner requires only minimal supervision and is not a threat to the public, he or she should be allowed to go home at regular intervals. This is a privilege which prisoners value and which, if they are properly selected, they are not likely to abuse. In the United States all but a few states operate a home leave system, the number of days allowed ranging from one to thirty. Prisoners in Sweden become eligible for home leave after serving four to six months and life sentence prisoners after two years. In Canada regular three-day leaves are allowed after one fifth of a sentence has been served, and roughly 15 per cent of prisoners serving over two years are on temporary release at any one time. Similar arrangements exist in many other countries.

When the threat which an individual prisoner presents to society is such that he or she cannot be allowed out of prison, proper arrangements should be made to maintain family ties within the prison setting. The arrangements made in many prisons in central and eastern Europe are a good example of what is possible. Prisoners are allowed to receive regular visits, usually lasting between two and four hours, in a formal visiting room. Within each prison there are several small flats where prisoners may receive family visits lasting up to 72 hours three times a year. It is not uncommon to find three generations of family visiting one prisoner. The visitors bring their own food and for a few days live as a family again. Much less use is made of these arrangements in the United Kingdom than in other countries.

There are other ways in which the isolation of the prison can be broken down. Low security prisoners can go into the community each day to learn trade skills or to work. They can make a contribution to society by working in a voluntary capacity with people who are more disadvantaged than they. There are also opportunities for people from the community to come into prison to work alongside prisoners or to make use of the facilities which some prisons have. These are not soft options. They are a real way of giving prisoners a sense of their own worth as human beings and showing them that they have talents and skills which they can use for the advantage of others.

Legally the responsibility of the prison system for people who are in prison ends when they pass through the gate at the end of sentence. It is generally accepted now that a major task of any prison system is to prepare prisoners for release. If this is done properly the man or woman who is released back into the community will be more likely to become a law-abiding member of that community.

Preparation for release can take many forms. In the case of a person who has been in prison for many years it may be a matter of helping the person to come to terms with all the changes which have taken place in society. In the early 1970s, for example, long-term prisoners due for release were quite confused about the new decimal currency which had been introduced some years previously. There are many stories of grown men and women being taken for a day out with a member of staff shortly before coming to the end of a long sentence, standing shaking at the kerbside unable to cross a busy street without encouragement from their companion.

For many prisoners preparation for release may take the form of learning the basic survival skills of how to live alone, how to budget on a small income, to cook healthy food, to wash and iron. Some prisoners from Brixton now go on short team-building exercises in the countryside, living on land owned by the prison service. One of the officers who goes along with these prisoners was quite sceptical initially about the value of such exercises, suspecting that it would be little more than a holiday for the prisoners. On return from the first such expedition he went out of his way to let his colleagues know that he had changed his view. Prisoners had learned to survive on their own and to recognize that they needed other people and were needed by them. In a relaxed environment of an evening they talked about many important issues in their lives which would never have been discussed in prison.

Several large companies now send representatives into prisons such as Brixton on a regular basis to coach prisoners on how to apply for jobs, on how to present oneself at interview, on how to deal with the matter of previous convictions, on how to cope with the failure which may well come.

Prisoners sentenced to twelve months or more in prison now receive support and supervision on release from probation officers.

BRIXTON 2000: A LONG-TERM STRATEGY

Brixton, like many large local prisons, had developed a capacity of which staff were proud, to cope well with the problems of each day. It was not good at planning ahead, to prevent problems which might arise and to take charge of its own destiny. It was assumed that it had no alternative but to be demand-led. Once the immediate problems of late 1991 had been dealt with the next requirement was for senior management to stand back from the daily grind and to draw up the structure of a strategic plan which would allow the prison and those who worked in it to identify the need for change and to take charge of its direction and pace.

This process required a great deal of commitment at all levels. The broad parameters of the plan were drawn up by senior management. They were then shared with all staff. Each group was encouraged to put flesh on the skeleton in respect of its own area of work. What emerged was 'Brixton 2000'. This strategic plan was underpinned by a vision and a set of shared values which all staff were asked to take on board. They included:

- The provision of appropriate custody in safe and decent conditions.
- Openness, fairness and justice.
- The need to establish high quality standards.
- The high commitment of Brixton staff.
- The commitment of management to staff.
- Trained staff who would provide programmes which offered prisoners opportunity and dignity.
- Sharing and supporting in difficult tasks by using a team approach.
- Providing opportunities for staff and for prisoners.
- Positive relationships between staff and prisoners which would be the key to a high quality of custody, care and justice.

These were not the sort of words which were in general use in a large local prison which concentrated all its efforts on getting through the business of the day. But they struck a chord with many staff. This underlined the fact that often management sets staff too low a standard and can legitimately expect more of them. The response of staff also demonstrated that management had to learn to trust staff more and to allow them to make use of the skills which many of them possessed.

There is still a long way to go in Brixton Prison. The distance which has already been travelled was recognized by the same Chief Inspector of Prisons who described Brixton in his 1990 inspection report as 'a corrupting and depressing institution'. In the report of his 1992 inspection[15] he charted a remarkable improvement, summed up by the comment made to him by one prisoner:

> The difference in this nick from two years ago is that staff now show us some respect.

REFERENCES

1. HM Chief Inspector of Prisons (1990), Report of an Inspection of HM Prison Brixton, Home Office, London.
2. Council of Europe (1991), Report to the United Kingdom Government on the Visit to the United Kingdom carried out by the European Committee for the Prevention of Torture and Inhuman or Degrading Treatment or Punishment, Council of Europe, Strasbourg.
3. Gunn, J et al. (1991), 'Mentally Disordered Prisoners', Home Office, London.
4. Grounds, A et al. (1991), Mentally Disordered Remand Prisoners, Home Office, London.
5. Department of Health & Home Office (1992), Review of Health and Social Services for Mentally Disordered Offenders and Others Requiring Similar Services, HMSO, London, Cmnd 2088.
6. *Race and the Criminal Justice System: A Home Office publication under section 95 of the Criminal Justice Act 1991* (1992), The Home Office, London.
7. Terminology in the context of race is both difficult and sensitive. The term 'ethnic minority' is used in government surveys as a generic description of people who are black or Asian. The term 'black' is also sometimes used in a generic sense.

8.   Hood, R (1992), *Race and Sentencing*, Clarendon Press, Oxford.
9.   Office of Population Censuses and Surveys (1992), The National Prison Survey 1991, HMSO, London.
10. Report of HM Chief Inspector of Prisons April 1992–March 1993 (1993), HMSO, London.
11. Report of an Inquiry into Prison Disturbances April 1990 (1991), HMSO, London, Cmnd 1456.
12. Report on the Work of the Prison Service: April 1991–March 1992 (1992), HMSO, London, Cmnd 2087.
13. HM Chief Inspector of Prisons (1990), Report of a Review of Suicide and Self-harm in England and Wales, HMSO, London, Cmnd 1383.
14. Americas Watch (1989), Prison Conditions in Brazil, Human Rights Watch, New York.
15. HM Chief Inspector of Prisons (1993), Report of an Inspection of HM Prison, Brixton, Home Office, London.

NINE

Prisoners of the System

MY BROTHER'S KEEPER

When a retirement party is held for a long-serving prison official anywhere in the world there will invariably be reference to 'having served two life sentences' or to 'getting out on parole' or to 'having earned good time'. There is many a true word spoken in jest.

The vast majority of prisoners are serving relatively short sentences and will soon leave prison behind. Many prison staff will spend their entire working lives, twenty, thirty or more years, behind bars. It takes a particular sort of person to earn his or her livelihood by locking up fellow human beings. What kind of people do such a job? Do they have to be particularly insensitive to the sufferings of others? Do they consider themselves to be guardians of society, protecting it from people who threaten its foundations? Are they men and women who are themselves insecure and who need a disciplined environment in which to work? Are they drawn, as some suggest, from the same background as the prisoners whom they guard, wearing a different uniform merely from force of circumstances? Are they fired with a sense of vocation, a mission to reform and to help fellow human beings? Or are they simply men and women doing a job of work, a task which pays the monthly bills and which is no different from any other?

Locking people up has never been a terribly reputable profession. In most communities it was traditionally carried out by a low-level public servant. It might be that the parish constable took it on as part of his general law-keeping obligations. In the 1830s the newly appointed Inspector of Prisons found that the jailer at Alloa in Scotland combined his duties with that of local chimney sweep. The Inspector dryly commented, 'Judging from his appearance, I should presume that he carries on an extensive business.'

Arrangements for keeping prisoners in custody were generally very disorganized. It might be, for example, that prisoners were responsible for providing their own food and drink. If they were lucky the wife of the jailer might supply some food at a cost. Otherwise the jailer would arrange for food and drink and other comforts to be sent in for payment. The report from the Inspector of Prisons on his inspection of Glasgow Gaol in 1838[1] paints a sorry picture:

> It seems to me proved that garnish is frequently exacted, and that prisoners are often ill-treated who refuse to pay it; that prisoners often pawn their clothes and steal from one another; that some of the servants of the gaol have assisted in conveying articles to the pawn shop.

It was not unusual that this garnish, as it was known, was the main source of income for the jailer. Rather than receive a salary it was not unknown for officials to pay for the privilege of taking over the running of particularly profitable prisons. In the middle ages the Fleet Prison in London had a carefully graduated scale of fees.[2]

Some of the severest criticisms levelled by the Inpsectors of Prisons who were first appointed by the government in 1835 to report on all places of detention were reserved for the staff whom they found running the prisons. They made the appointment of suitable staff and their subsequent training a high priority.

INTERNAL DIVISION

In the course of the nineteenth century it became increasingly common for retired officers from the armed services to be appointed as prison governors. This was due in no small part to the number of superannuated officers who were looking for public appointments after the end of the Napoleonic Wars. Much of the extensive programme of new prison building during this period was entrusted to officers of the Royal Engineers and several of them rose to key positions in the prison service. With the establishment of the Directorate of Convict Prisons in 1850 this tradition of appointing former army officers to senior positions was confirmed.

It was not surprising that these officers should have a tendency to appoint former members of the armed services as warders. It was logical that men schooled in the discipline of military service should be attracted to the new prisons which were to be run according to a hierarchical model which they knew well. By 1876 over two thirds of the subordinate officers employed in prisons were former servicemen. This tradition was to set the tone of the prison system in England and Wales for many years. It is a legacy which, for good and ill, has left its mark until the present time.

Sir Edmund du Cane, who became first Chairman of the Prison Commissioners of England and Wales in 1877, was promoted to the rank of major general in the Royal Engineers several years later. His opinion of the value of former servicemen to the prison service was echoed by many of his colleagues:

> Their habits of order and discipline, of rendering and enforcing strict obedience and their aptitude in dealing with large bodies of men, are unquestionably very valuable qualities for the office, and if not possessed by an officer on joining, would have to be acquired more or less perfectly afterwards. [3]

Not everyone, however, was happy with this model of the prison service. A contrary view was that the rigid military-style discipline which was enforced could easily spill over into brutality. In the early days of the enforced separation of prisoners it was not uncommon that prisoners were driven insane by the rigid discipline.

The dangers of inflexible discipline were brought to public attention after the report of the Gladstone Committee in 1895. [4] Thereafter there was a significant change of emphasis in the English prison service, particularly in the treatment of younger prisoners within the borstal system. This was achieved partly by direct recruitment to junior governor posts, known at the time as 'housemasters' in the public school tradition, of men who were in tune with the new principles and who

> by leadership and understanding were to help
> strengthen a boy's character, to encourage loyalty, trust
> and esprit de corps, and to develop any latent ability for
> leadership. [5]

The relationship between management and staff in the prison service in England and Wales has been heavily influenced by its historical antecedents. The work of the jailer carried a social stigma which set the holder of the post apart from the rest of society, somehow linked in the minds of others with the criminals for whom he was responsible. In the nineteenth century, with the growth of the imprisonment industry, senior posts were taken over by gentlemen and former army officers who were at pains to keep their distance from junior staff. As belief in the rehabilitative potential of imprisonment grew, greater attention was paid to the prisoner, to providing him with decent accommodation, with education and with other facilities which might benefit him on release. Well-meaning volunteers, many of them friends of the governor, took an interest in the prisoners and often made arrangements to help them when they had completed their sentences.

Staff contrasted this with the treatment which they received. Held in low regard by the public, they felt undervalued by management. The best the Earl of Stanhope could say when he investigated the work of the prison officer in 1923 was that he was 'especially impressed with the monotony of his life'. Prison officers were subject to a discipline similar to that of the armed forces and the police but they did not have the benefit of public esteem which the others enjoyed.

As a consequence of this prison staff turned in on themselves for mutual support. This became even more exaggerated when official staff quarters were provided. After the centralization of the prison system in 1877 it became common for staff to be transferred from prison to prison. This was made much easier since there was no need to find accommodation. This meant that not only did staff look to each other for support, but also the social lives of their families revolved around the prison. It was no surprise that the

May Committee of Inquiry noted that 'we have found members of the service (including governors) a somewhat inward-looking group'.[6]

The insularity of prison staff has found its voice over the last fifty years in the activity of the Prison Officers' Association. It came into being despite the active opposition of management and today is described as one of the last of the old-style reactionary trade unions. If this is true, it is as much a reflection on the way management in the prison service has treated its staff as it is on the staff themselves. The majority of prison officers are members of the POA. The sort of men and women who join a disciplined service are not natural activists. It is the misfortune of the prison service that they have become so.

James Jacobs, an eminent commentator on prison matters in the United States, has described how prison administrators in that country continue to see staff unions as 'a mortal enemy', intent on usurping their legitimate authority. In the middle years of the twentieth century that was almost how prison management viewed the POA. The union responded with similar mistrust.

NEW STRUCTURES

Since staff felt that their work was not valued as it should have been they sought recompense in a much more practical way. The first fifty years of existence of the POA were marked by a regular set of claims for increased pay. These were met by a succession of offical enquiries which produced settlements of varying generosity. Since the basic pay rates of prison staff were linked to civil service administrative pay, officers and management colluded over the years to make increasing use of overtime payments.

By the mid 1980s this had reached an impossible situation with overtime payments accounting for almost one third of the salary bill. This arrangement satisfied no one. Officers were discontented that they had to work so many hours overtime to earn what they considered to be a decent wage. Management was frustrated by the demand-led nature of work and the rigid staffing levels which provided staff with a set of arcane working practices which guaranteed virtually unlimited overtime.

Over a number of years there had also been a growing

perception that there were too many different grades within the staff structure. Specifically, there was an overlap at middle management level. The junior grades of governor were technically senior to the chief officer grades but they had markedly less experience and in many instances less credibility with junior staff.

The Home Office produced a set of radical proposals to deal with these issues. This was known as 'Fresh Start'. It consisted of new working arrangements which did away with overtime, a reorganized management structure and a unification of the governor and prison officer grades. These changes were linked to a new system covering pay and conditions of service.

THE ROLE OF THE PRISON OFFICER

The dissatisfaction of staff may have been focused on matters of pay but the frustration had been also about the quality of work which was expected of the prison officer and the extent to which initiative was discouraged. In 1963 the POA issued a memorandum on the Role of the Modern Prison Officer. This was a positive document which described in detail how the association wished to see the role of the prison officer developed. The subject was pursued with unfailing regularity at the annual conferences of the association.

With the exception of work carried out in some borstal institutions with young offenders, the tasks assigned to staff were generally mundane. In 1921 their title had been changed from warder to prison officer but the change had been one in name only. New staff, assistant governors, probation officers, teachers and psychologists were recruited to take care of the positive side of work with prisoners. The basic task of the prison officer remained that of ensuring that prisoners were in the right place at the right time.

Since the introduction of the Fresh Start arrangements in 1987 genuine efforts have been made to develop the work of the prison officer. This makes sense for several reasons. Prison officers are the people closest to the prisoners. They unlock the cells first thing in the morning and lock them last thing at night. In between they see the prisoners when they are at their best and when they are at their worst, when they are strongest and when they are weakest. There is a symbiotic relationship between the prisoner and the prison officer. One cannot exist without the other. The prison officer is the person in the system who knows most about the prisoner and who is likely to have the greatest influence on him or her.

Procedures have now been set up to ensure that all prisoners have a set of short-term objectives which will help them through their sentences and which will eventually prepare them for release. These objectives are described as a sentence plan. The key player in this arrangement, in helping the prisoner to work out this plan, is the officer who looks after him or her each day on the landing. Officers are now encouraged to get to know the individual prisoners under their charge. Prisoners are expected to discuss personal matters with their landing officers. A far cry from the days when officers wore cutlasses and prisoners were not allowed to come closer than a drawn cutlass-length.

TRAINING PRISON STAFF

Professional training plays a central role in establishing the status of any group of workers. In this respect it took many years before the need for formal training of prison staff was recognized. Until the time of the Gladstone Committee in 1895 warders were given 'on the job' training. In theory they were required to work alongside experienced staff for the first three months and were not allowed to take charge of prisoners during that period. The reality, particularly in local prisons, was that shortage of staff frequently meant that trainee officers were required to carry out duties unsupervised.

The report of the Gladstone Committee[7] was the first major report to indentify the need for formal training for prison staff. In due course the Imperial Training School for Warders was established at Wakefield Prison and all new recruits to the prison service were required to undergo a period of training and testing lasting two months. The initial training of recruit prison officers has changed little in length and not a great deal in content over the last sixty years. Very recently the requirement to undertake training in basic drill techniques has been abolished and much more attention is paid to 'interpersonal skills'.

The new prison officer now has to pass through a probationary year, which includes the nine weeks which he or she spends at the training college. For the rest of the year the officer is under the supervision of a training officer at the prison to which he or she is posted. During this time it is expected that the new officer will attend various short courses in the prison. In future years there will be the opportunity, but not the obligation, to attend other short courses at the training college.

Until 1987 men and women who were appointed as assistant governors, either from the ranks of prison officers or directly to the service, underwent a two-year training course, based partly at the training college and partly in prisons. This form of recruitment and training has now been discontinued in England and Wales. Promotion is achieved progressively through the ranks, beginning at officer level. There are already indications of a need to recruit fresh blood at management level and there is a general expectation that this will be reintroduced before long.

THE MOST IMPORTANT ASSET OF THE PRISON SERVICE[8]

There is a most remarkable dichotomy within the Prison Service. The dichotomy is between:

i) the high calibre and deep commitment of the majority of Prison Service staff, at all levels. They have an immense sense of loyalty. They have a warm sense of camaraderie with their colleagues. They want to see improvements within the prison system; and

ii) the dissension, division and distrust which exist between all levels of Prison Service staff. They labour under a blanket of depression. They lack confidence in the value of what they do. They harbour a deep sense of frustration that the effort which they are devoting to the Service is not appreciated.[9]

In this clearly expressed paragraph Lord Justice Woolf went to the heart of the malaise which has infected the prison service in England and Wales for many years. Its staff are by temperament loyal and willing to follow decisive leadership. They have consistently felt that they have not been given this. They have concluded that management is more concerned at improving the lot of the prisoner than in making best use of its staff. As a consequence they have turned inwards and their energies have been largely expended in a frustrated resistance to change.

The vicious circle which this has created was indentified in a recent report on the management of the prison service:

> Difficult unions fill the vacuum left by ineffective management and all managements are ineffective if they are not allowed to manage. [10]

It is sometimes argued that the distrust which exists between all levels in the prison service results from the fact that the service has until recently been located within the central machinery of the civil service, a machinery better attuned to advising ministers of government than to executive management. This is too simple to be a complete answer. The divisions within prisons between staff and management existed during the lifetime of the Prison Commission.

There is a clear expectation that the move to agency status, with the increased autonomy which that brings, will lead to greater integration of the various sections within the prison service. The statement of value that staff are the most important asset of the prison service is intended to be a clear indicator of this change. There is a long tradition of 'dissension, division and distrust' to be reversed. It remains to be seen whether this legacy can be overcome in the prison service of England and Wales.

INTERNATIONAL COMPARISONS

Across the world the major issues affecting prison staff are broadly similar, varying from country to country only in degree of importance. Work as a prison officer, as a guard, as a correctional worker, however it is described, is invariably seen to be at the lower end of law enforcement. First-line prison staff often compare themselves to policemen. In reality this parallel is not accepted by their employers or by the public. The exception is when, as happens in some of the United States of America, town and county jails are the responsibility of the local sheriff and policemen take a spell of duty as guards in these prisons.

In several countries militarism is explicit. This may include the ranking structure of staff and their designation. In eastern Europe and the countries of the former Soviet Union staff have military rank and, as members of the Ministry of the Interior, form part of what is in effect the internal armed forces. This structure undoubtedly affects the relationship between staff and the prisoners. In Communist times prisoners were class enemies and were not thought to have any human rights. They were regarded very much as non-people.

Even in countries where the staff structure is not directly military there is often a clear distinction between senior and junior members of staff. The former are known as directors, governors or wardens and consider themselves to be quite separate from the 'other ranks' who deal directly with prisoners.

In several of the former Soviet countries, including Russia, there is a genuine desire at senior levels to observe universal norms and guidelines and to respect prisoners as individuals. It is difficult to translate these priniciples into practice in a system grounded in a philosphy which does not regard the prisoner as a person. Inevitably in such systems many staff will have been compromised by their previous behaviour or at least will be unable to adjust to the new regime. As standards changed in the prison system in Poland, one third of the 20,000 staff left the service in the sixteen months up to January 1992. Speaking in September 1993 the Director General of the Prison Service of the Czech Republic was quite explicit:

> As changes took place it was necessary to remove those prison staff who were compromised by direct participation in the injustices which had taken place during the previous regime. In Czechoslovakia, for example, out of a total staff of 7500 people, 1500 were fired. [11]

There is a real danger in a prison system that staff come to regard themselves as better human beings than the prisoners in their charge and that this is reflected in the way they treat them. In some prison systems this attitude is unspoken but none the less present. In others it is quite explicit. A report of prison conditions in Nigeria[12] comments:

For the custodians of Nigeria's penal tombs, the very fact of imprisonment, by some easy but untenable logic, strips a man or woman of the inherent quality of humanity.

One problem in many countries is that prison staff are little respected by the public and very poorly paid. The same report on Nigerian prisons recognizes the difficult position in which staff find themselves:

The guardians of the 363 prisons and lock-ups in Nigeria probably have the worst conditions of service among government workers in the whole of the country. Despised and neglected, the warders of Nigeria's prisons are made unable to do the job which society has assigned to them.

Given that many prisons are situated in isolated areas, far from the centres of population, it is little wonder that staff become insular and that their isolation from the rest of society becomes exaggerated.

In some countries staff are given extensive training before taking up duty. In Denmark, for example, the initial training of staff lasts three years, a combination of college courses and supervised placements in prisons. This contrasts with other countries where training for recruits lasts little more than a few weeks. The Federal Bureau of Prisons in the United States, for example, provides an initial three-week training programme for all staff. Elsewhere training is virtually non-existent and new staff are expected to learn from their more experienced colleagues.

The relationship between staff and prisoners and the role of the prison officer is to some extent determined by the ratio of one to the other. It is not uncommon in prisons in the United Kingdom that one officer on a landing takes care of twenty prisoners. This means that he or she has the opportunity to get to know them as individuals, their personal strengths and weaknesses, and to be able to offer assistance with problems. In prisons in the former Soviet Union one officer may be looking after anything up to 200 prisoners, confined in large dormitories. In such a setting it is difficult to be much more than a guard who simply counts heads.

Even in such a setting it is possible to set some standard of human respect. I recall witnessing two very different incidents which underlined that fact. Butyrka Prison in Moscow is a penal monster, designed to hold 3,500 prisoners and now regularly holding in excess of 5,000. Cells built for 40 men hold more than 70. When being shown round by the colonel in charge we entered one over-crowded and foetid cell. The colonel was immediately surrounded by a group of men animatedly demanding response to various questions. He responded equally vigorously. It was obvious that they knew the colonel personally and that they were not afraid to raise matters of concern directly with him.

The second incident took place in the main prison in Banjul in the Gambia. Physical conditions were very basic and facilities were limited. The prisoners put on a concert of local dance for the group of visiting dignitaries. Suddenly the Commissioner of Prisons left the group of visitors and energetically joined in the dance to the great delight of the prisoners who clearly knew him well. In both these incidents senior prison officials were demonstrating by their example to junior staff that it was possible to treat prisoners with respect without losing authority.

CONCLUSION

Among the many words which have been written about prisons and prisoners comparatively little attention has been paid to the prison officer. It is as though he or she is a cog in the great machine, necessary for its smooth running but virtually unnoticed. The reality is that the prison officer is the key to the good management of any prison and the most important person in respect of the treatment of prisoners. Instructions may float down from head office, orders may emanate from the governor's office, but it is the prison officer on the landing or in the compound who will determine the real quality of life for the prisoner. It is the officer who unlocks the prisoner in the morning. It is the officer who locks him up at night. It is the officer who is with him at all times in between. Prisoners are well aware of this. All other people concerned with prisons, politicians, administrators, academics, would do well to remember it.

If we expect prisoners to behave decently and in accordance with the law once they have been released, they must be treated in a similar fashion while they are in prison. If we expect staff to treat prisoners humanely and with respect for their rights, they in turn must be treated in a similar manner by their own management and by society.

REFERENCES

1. Report of Inspector of Prisons for Scotland (1839), HMSO, London.
2. cf. McConville, S (1981), *A History of English Prison Administration, Vol I: 1750–1877*, Routledge & Kegan Paul, London.
3. Quoted in Thomas, J E (1972), *The English Prison Officer Since 1850: A Study in Conflict*, Routledge & Kegan Paul, London.
4. Report from the Departmental Committee on Prisons (1895), HMSO, London, Cmnd 7702.
5. Grew, B D (1958), *Prison Governor*, Herbert Jenkins, London.
6. Report of the Committee of Inquiry into the United Kingdom Prison Services (1979), HMSO, London, Cmnd 7673.
7. Report from the Departmental Committee on Prisons (1895), HMSO, London, Cmnd 7702.
8. The second value of the Prison Service of England and Wales as expressed in its Corporate Plan for 1993–1996.
9. Report of an Inquiry into Prison Disturbances April 1990 (1991), HMSO, London, Cmnd 1456, para. 12.1.
10. Report by Sir Raymond Lygo on the Management of the Prison Service (1991), Home Office, London.
11. Karabec, Z (1993), 'Problems of a Prison System in a Period of Transition Towards Democracy', A Paper presented at a Seminar on Reform of the Criminal Law and the Prison System held in Bishkek, Kyrgyzstan, September 1993.
12. Civil Liberties Organization (1991), 'Behind the Wall: A Report on Prison Conditions in Nigeria', Civil Liberties Organization, Nigeria.

TEN

The Woolf Report
and After

On Sunday morning, 1 April 1990, the church service in Strangeways Prison in Manchester, England, was coming to an end when a prisoner walked to the front of the chapel and took hold of the microphone.

> He began to address the congregation, talking about the hardness of the prison system. A tape recording was made of this part of the service and fortunately it survived the subsequent disturbance. This gives the best indication of what was happening. It makes clear that pandemonium broke out.[1]

So began the Strangeways prison riot, the worst in English prison history. When it ended 25 days later, one prisoner had died in circumstances which may have been connected with the disturbance. One officer had died of pneumonia. Later another prisoner who had played a prominent part in the riot took his life in another establishment. 47 prisoners were injured. 147 members of staff received injuries or were affected by smoke or fumes. The cost of repairing the blackened shell of what remained of the prison was estimated at £60 millions. For 25 days television pictures had flashed across the world showing prisoners systematically destroying the prison, standing defiantly on the roof to taunt the authorities. In the early days of April 1990 there were major disturbances at six other prisons in England and Wales as well as a number of incidents in other prisons.

What had gone wrong, that prisoners had engaged in such a sustained orgy of violence, which everyone knew would eventually be brought to an end with the ringleaders receiving long additional sentences of imprisonment? On 6 April 1990, while the riot at Strangeways was still in progress, the Home Secretary appointed an eminent judge, the then Lord Justice Woolf, to carry out an inquiry.

Lord Woolf's terms of reference were to inquire into the events leading up to the riot at Manchester and at the other prisons where disturbances occurred and at the way they were dealt with. As had happened with previous prison inquiries,[2] Woolf decided at an early stage that he would have to expand his terms of reference considerably to take account of 'the underlying problems of the prison service) and the remedies which they require' (para. 1.12).

The report which Woolf submitted to the Home Secretary on 31 January 1991 is a seminal document which, in its own words, erects a series of signposts (para. 1.8) which the prison service must follow if it is to achieve its stated objectives. The signposts are expressed in a language which can be understood in any country and in any prison administration.

PREVIOUS PRISON INQUIRIES

A unified national prison service was established in England and Wales by the Prisons Act of 1877. Since then the prison system has been the subject of several major independent inquiries. The frequency of these inquiries increased significantly as the twentieth century progressed.

In 1894 the Gladstone Committee was asked to report on the administration of prisons and the treatment and classification of prisoners. Its report the following year[3] included the famous dictum:

> we start from the principle that prison treatment should
> have as its primary and concurrent objects, deterrence,
> and reformation.

The confusion which arose from this dictum, based on the illogical premise that there can ever be two primary principles, led directly to many of the difficulties in which prison systems in the United Kingdom and elsewhere have found themselves throughout the twentieth century.

In 1923 the Stanhope Committee was appointed to investigate the pay and conditions of service for prison staff. For fifty years prison officers had been pressing for parity of pay with the police. The Committee was not convinced by their arguments. The Stanhope Report[4] concluded that existing pay scales for officers were adequate both in relation to the nature of their work and the type of man they were meant to attract. At the same time it recommended significant pay rises for prison governors. This report and the boost which it gave to the clandestine staff association which was eventually to become the Prison Officers Association did much to sow the seeds of future staff industrial relations difficulties in the prison service.

On 24 January 1931 prisoners in Dartmoor Prison rioted. The mutiny was suppressed by prison officers using firearms, assisted by police. Herbert du Parq KC was appointed to inquire into the riot. The evidence given to the inquiry was never published although its report was. In this[5] du Parq concluded that a small number of officers had been guilty of 'irregularities and worse'. He dismissed suggestions that the mutiny had been due to the 'humane' treatment of prisoners. Alexander Paterson, the most influential Prison Commissioner of the time, assisted du Parq in his inquiry. J. E. Thomas[6] has suggested that it was due to pressure from Paterson that du Parq did not recognize that the consequences of reform, which allowed prisoners to communicate and to organize themselves, had indeed contributed significantly to the riot.

Continuing staff dissatisfaction with their terms of employment led in 1957 to the appointment of the Wynn Parry Committee to inquire into the pay and conditions of service of prison staff. The report of the committee[7] expressed the view that the prison service was 'sui generis'. This description was seized on by prison governors, particularly in respect of their relationships with administrative grade civil servants.

The Wynn Parry Report also went out of its way to comment unfavourably on the treatment which it saw being meted out to staff in contrast to that given to prisoners.

In short we saw living and working conditions which can only be described as Dickensian. Substantial improvements have been made for the prison population with the emphasis now on training and rehabilitation, but in our view parallel improvements have not been made for the staff.

This perception was, and to a certain extent still is, shared by staff and has affected some of their reaction to proposed developments in regimes for prisoners.

In the early 1960s a series of spectacular escapes from English prisons occurred. J. E. Thomas[8] has argued that these escapes were merely the culmination of the general confusion which existed among prison staff at all levels as to the primary aim of the prison service, a confusion which had its roots in the Gladstone Report of 1895. The final straw was the escape of the spy George Blake, who was serving a prison sentence of 42 years, from Wormwood Scrubs Prison on 22 October 1966. Two days after this incident Earl Mountbatten of Burma was appointed to inquire into this and other recent prison escapes and to make recommendations for the improvement of prison security.

The Mountbatten Report[9] was published in December 1966. It is a remarkably precise document which addressed itself directly to its terms of reference. In respect of security the report contained two main recommendations. The first was that all prisoners should be allocated to one of four security categories, which would be in descending order A, B, C and D. This recommendation was accepted and has been in operation since then.

The second security recommendation was that a new super-secure prison should be built on the Isle of Wight and that all prisoners in the highest security category should be held there. This recommendation was rejected by the government. Two years later the Radzinowicz Committee[10] recommended that long-term prisoners who required to be held in conditions of maximum security should be dispersed throughout a number of highly secure prisons. The Radzinowicz recommendation was implemented and has had a fundamental influence on the subsequent development of the long-term prison system in England and Wales.

Mountbatten did not overlook the fact that keeping prisoners positively and constructively occupied would lead to an improvement in security:

> The nature of the prison regime itself can also contribute greatly to the reduction of the kind of tensions that turn prisoners' minds towards escape. Occupation with worthwhile work, a firm but humane governor and staff, and reasonable opportunities for constructive recreation are not only desirable in themselves but will make for better security. The closer the relationship between prisoners and staff, and the more the majority of prisoners accept the fairness of their treatment, the easier it will be to detect symptoms of unrest which often indicate the planning of an escape attempt (para. 322).

The political consequences of the highly publicized escapes in the 1960s meant that the main effect of the Mountbatten Report was that security considerations weighed much more heavily with the prison service in the latter years of the twentieth century than they had done since the Gladstone Report.

The prison system in England and Wales came under considerable pressure in the 1970s. This pressure was caused by an increasing number of prisoners, increasing staff militancy and an increased demand for prisoners' rights. The deteriorating state of industrial relations caused greatest concern to those within the system. On 27 October 1978 the English Prison Governors' Committee sent an open letter to the Home Secretary. It began:

> Total breakdown is imminent in the prison system. Prison Governors believe that it is our duty to publicly warn Ministers of the gravity of the situation we face. There is little time left.

The letter went on to argue that the root of the problem was an outdated and unworkable industrial relations structure, exacerbated by a 'deplorable lack of leadership from the Home Office'.

> We consider that the present chaotic situation demands

a rigorous public inquiry into industrial relations within the Prison Service.

The Home Secretary responded to this letter with a speed which surprised even the prison governors. On 6 November he announced that a wide-ranging committee of inquiry into the United Kingdom Prison Services would be set up. The May Report[11] was published in October 1979. Its extensive list of recommendations dealt with the size and nature of the prison population, objectives and regimes, the organization of the prison system, resources, the role, recruitment and training of staff, their pay and conditions of service and industrial relations.

The original impetus for the establishment of the May Committee had been the poor state of industrial relations in the prison service in England and Wales and a particular problem with payment of an allowance for prison officers. The committee recognized that it could not deal with these specific matters without taking on board the more fundamental problems facing the prison service. It attempted to analyse these in the time-honoured fashion of a government inquiry. It considered the voluminous evidence submitted by the relevant government departments. It took account of written and oral evidence from trades unions and other interested bodies. It then tried to write a comprehensive report and set of recommendations. All of this against a tight time scale.

As with most such committees, it argued that its report should be accepted as a package. The response of the government was less than whole hearted. The editorial in *The Scotsman* newspaper on 1 November 1979 was not surprised:

> This traditional public indifference to what goes on inside prisons (except when prisoners are alleged to be pampered) no doubt helps to explain why Mr Whitelaw, while he jumped into immediate acceptance of the pay recommendations by the Inquiry, was much more cautious about the prison-building and prison-reform programmes that were simultaneously recommended.

The May Committee dealt in the very short term, but not in the longer term, with the problem of staff pay for which it had been set up. It left very little else to show for its efforts. The notion of 'positive custody' which it advocated did not attract any support. The recommendation that the Prisons Board should have a chairman who would be the accounting officer for the prison service and who would have direct access to the Home Secretary disappeared without trace, although it is remarkably close to the changes which were introduced when the prison service became an agency on 1 April 1993. The reality was that in 1979 the time was not ripe for fundamental reform of the prison systems in the United Kingdom.

One of May's recommendations did have a far-reaching effect on prison reform in England and Wales. May recognized the need for some form of effective and independent inspection of the prison service. He concluded that, because the Home Secretary is ultimately accountable to parliament for the management of the prison service, it would not be possible to have a completely independent form of inspection. He recommended that a prisons inspectorate should be set up within the Home Office, 'distanced from it as far as may be practicable'. This recommendation was accepted. The Inspectorate as it has developed since its inception is now seen in the eyes of many commentators as something approaching a model for this kind of distanced watchdog body.

THE SIGNIFICANCE OF WOOLF

The nature of imprisonment in the United Kingdom in the twentieth century has been based on the philosophy described in the Gladstone Report published at the end of the nineteenth century. In broad terms this was that prison had to be strict enough to deter people from a life of crime but that its other main objective was to reform the prisoner so that he or she would be 'rehabilitated' by the experience of imprisonment. There was an assumption that a person who committed a crime must in some way have a personality weakness. If only this could be identified, the person could be cured, made whole again before return to the community. This philosophy, sometimes described as the medical model of imprisonment, was paternalistic: if only the prisoner would do as we told him or her, all would be well.

During the second half of the twentieth century there has been little real belief in this philosophy. It came from an age of greater confidence and reflected a certainty which had long ago been shown to be false. The facts showed that criminals were not deterred by the experience of imprisonment. Nor were they changed for the better. On the contrary, by that measurement prison was a failure. Many people left prison more likely to commit serious crime than when they went in.

As belief in the efficacy of prison waned, its use by the courts increased. There was confusion at many levels in the criminal justice system about why prison was being used and what it was meant to achieve. This confusion affected the management of the prison system. The Victorian philosophy of rehabilitation had been discredited but had not been replaced. Academics and others preached the message that 'nothing works'. In the long term men and women were little influenced by their experiences in prison. Therefore, there was little point in trying to achieve anything. The best that could be aimed for was to reduce the harm done to a person by imprisonment.

Whatever the academic merit of such an argument, it did little for the confidence of those who worked in the prison system. It led to uncertainty and confusion. There was a dissonance between theory and practice which led to a crisis of credibility. The various departmental inquiries referred to above were narrow in their terms of reference and concerned themselves only with particular areas of difficulty. Prison officers were aware of this vacuum as they went about their daily duties. They lost any sense of direction. They in turn passed inconsistent messages to prisoners.

The consequences of two generations of this inconsistency were there for all to see. A staff who were largely demoralized and who resorted to industrial action as much out of frustration as anything else. Prisoners who often felt that they were being treated unfairly and unjustly and who resorted increasingly to rioting and violence.

Strangeways in April 1990 was the ultimate riot in the prison history of the United Kingdom. The phoenix which arose out of its ashes was the report for which the prison system had been waiting for forty years.

HOW WOOLF WENT ABOUT HIS TASK

When the Woolf Report was published on 25 February 1991 it received unanimous praise. The reaction of the Chairman of the Prison Reform Trust was typical:

It constitutes a wide-ranging examination of conditions in Britain's gaols and is the most significant analysis of the penal system in a hundred years. The Report's 12 major recommendations and 204 proposals on matters of detail set out an agenda for a total overhaul of the prison system and will shape penal policy well into the next century.[12]

It is important to realize that Woolf was not a committee of inquiry. It was a departmental inquiry conducted by a judge, in other words, a judicial inquiry. Lord Justice Woolf alone was responsible for the first part of the report, which examined in detail the disturbances at six penal establishments during April 1990. He was joined by Judge Stephen Tumim, HM Chief Inspector of Prisons, in writing part two of the report which examines wider issues arising out of the disturbances. Woolf was assisted by three assessors. Woolf himself would be the first to recognize the contribution which the assessors, a recently retired Deputy Director General of the Prison Service, the former head of the Home Office Research and Planning Unit and a professor of criminal justice, made to the way in which his thinking on the issues at hand developed. But Woolf himself wrote the report and bears personal responsibility for it.

The Home Secretary made clear that he was content that Woolf should interpret his terms of reference in as broad a fashion as he saw necessary.[13] Woolf took full advantage of this and it has been suggested that the manner in which the inquiry was conducted could serve as a model which might usefully be followed by future inquiries.[14]

Woolf's method of working was guided by four principles. The first was that as far as possible the inquiry should be conducted in public. Given the secrecy surrounding much of what goes on in prisons, this was considered to be particularly important. The second principle was that the inquiry should be conducted on 'a broad canvas', identifying underlying problems and suggesting solutions. Thirdly, the inquiry should consult as widely as possible, not only official sources, but anyone who felt that he or she had something useful to contribute. Finally, the inquiry should be concluded with all possible speed.

In respect of the disturbances themselves, Woolf was at pains to ensure that anyone who had been directly involved should have the opportunity to comment, either orally or in writing. In addition to the large number of individual interviews which took place, Lord Woolf sent a personal letter to 1,350 members of staff and to 4,050 prisoners who had been in any of the six establishments at the time of the disturbances, inviting comment. He received 260 replies from prison staff and 600 from prisoners. He also wrote a general letter to all members of the prison service and another to all prisoners. Letters inviting comment also went to 95 individuals and organizations who it was thought might wish to contribute to the inquiry.

Oral evidence on matters relating to the first part of the inquiry, that is to do with the incidents, was taken at three hearings, in Manchester, Taunton and London. Most of this evidence was taken in public. In order to protect their identity, some prisoners were interviewed in private.

The normal procedure for inquiries such as that conducted by Lord Justice Woolf is that written submissions are considered in private session. The inquiry then invites some of those who have submitted written evidence to come individually or in groups representing a particular interest to give evidence in private. Woolf decided that this form of consultation was not sufficient. When it came to considering matters covered by the second part of the inquiry, those of more general importance, he decided to continue with the format of public hearings which he had used in respect of the first part of the inquiry.

Public seminars, each lasting two days, were arranged to discuss the tactical management of the prison population, active regimes, relationships with the criminal justice system, the administration of the prison service and justice in prisons. This was a new way of working for a judicial inquiry and its openness attracted a great deal of positive comment. There were concerns within the civil service that officials would be placed in the difficult position of having to express personal opinions on issues which were matters of government policy. For that reason Woolf adopted what one of his assessors[15] has called the 'transparently fictional device' of stating at the opening of each seminar that the civil servants who were present would be speaking as individuals and not as representatives of their departments.[16]

One criticism of the public seminars was that they did not

include any representation from prisoners. However, in October the Inquiry team held two short seminars in Lincoln Prison, one for prisoners and one for staff. In the course of the inquiry Lord Justice Woolf visited 43 prisons in the United Kingdom and elsewhere, taking the opportunity to speak to both staff and prisoners.

The message at the heart of the Woolf Report is confirmed by the way in which the inquiry went about its business. By the manner in which he conducted the inquiry Lord Justice Woolf underlined his view that prisons are an integral part of the criminal justice process and that justice must not stop at the prison gate. He also emphasized that there must be a close link between the prison and the community which it serves. If this link is broken, if the community is excluded from discussion about and responsibility for what goes on in prisons, the likelihood of instability within prisons will remain.

SECURITY, CONTROL AND JUSTICE

Having considered all the evidence which was submitted to him, Woolf concluded that a stable prison system will be built on three pillars: security, control and justice (para. 9.19). By *security*, he meant the obligation which a prison system has to protect the public by making sure that prisoners in its charge do not escape. Those who live or work in a prison are entitled to expect that prisons will be safe places. That means that prison systems must ensure that sufficient *control* is exercised over prisoners who are likely to be disruptive. Prisoners must be treated with humanity and fairness and be helped to prepare for their return to the community. Woolf encapsulates these concepts in the notion of *justice*.

If a prison system is to be genuinely stable, the importance of each of these three elements must be recognized. If one of them is ignored or given lesser priority, the system will become unstable. The large number of prisoners who gave evidence to Woolf expressed the opinion in one form or another that the need for justice was often overlooked in the prison system in England and Wales (para. 9.24). The report makes it quite clear that Woolf had a great deal of sympathy with this view. One of the main objectives of the recommendations which he made was to ensure that a prisoner serves his sentence in a way which is consistent with the purpose behind the Court's decision to take away his liberty and his freedom of movement, while ensuring he is treated with humanity and justice. (para. 14.5).

TOWARDS A CRIMINAL JUSTICE SYSTEM

Woolf recognized that no prison system exists in a vacuum. Its only justification for existence is to serve the wish of society, as expressed by the courts, to deprive certain individuals of their liberty. The criminal justice process begins when an offence is committed. It will be investigated by the police, who may make a charge against one or more people. The Crown Prosecution Service will decide whether to proceed with this charge and, if they do, will then prepare the prosecution case. Defence lawyers will normally prepare the case for the person who is accused. The case will be heard in open court and, if the person is found guilty, the judge will pass sentence. This may involve some form of penalty, such as a fine or supervision order. In this case the Probation Service may supervise the person who has been convicted while the penalty is being served. If the offence is so serious that there is no alternative or if the safety of the public requires it,[17] the judge will pass a sentence of imprisonment.

The various elements of the criminal justice process should be interlinked. In the United Kingdom they operate in such an autonomous manner that it is difficult to describe them as parts of a system. In many countries there is a closer link between all or some parts of the process. Sometimes this takes the form of a ministry or department of justice. In other instances the parts of the process which deal with executing penalties on the offender, such as probation, prison and parole, come under one umbrella. Such links have to do primarily with the administration of the system of justice and do not threaten the independence of any one part, such as the judiciary. They do ensure that no one element operates in isolation.

In recent years there has been increasing support for the view that there should be a genuine criminal justice *system* in England and Wales, probably under the umbrella of a Ministry of Justice. There is as yet no official support for this position although there are practical indications of a move in this direction. Responsibility for administration of magistrates' courts, for example, was passed from the Home Office to the Lord Chancellor's Department in 1992 and a junior government minister in the House of Commons now deals with matters affecting the Lord Chancellor's Department.

Woolf was very conscious of the need for greater cooperation among the various parts of the criminal justice process and for the prison system to be recognized as an integral part of that process (para. 1.156). He described the lack of cooperation as a major geological fault (para. 10.169). To have recommended anything like a ministry of justice would have exceeded his terms of reference in a way which would have been unacceptable. What he did recommend was that a national forum should be set up within which matters of common interest to the various parts of the criminal justice process could be discussed and proposals for improvement could be considered (para. 1.170). There should also be local committees of a similar nature.

The government accepted this recommendation. A national Criminal Justice Consultative Council, chaired by a senior judge, has been set up, as have 24 area committees.

VISIBLE LEADERSHIP

In his analysis of the management of the various prison disturbances which took place in April 1990 Woolf commented adversely on the lack of visible leadership which was shown in several instances (para. 1.173). The lack of obvious leadership was felt generally throughout the prison service. This was attributed at least in part to the fact that the Director General was an administrative civil servant who saw his chief responsibilities as being for policy and for advising government ministers rather than for managing the prison service (para. 12.27).

This lack of clear leadership had been identified as a major problem in 1966 by Earl Mountbatten in his inquiry into prison escapes. Mountbatten had concluded that there was a need for a professional head of the prison service who would give leadership to the service and who would be recognized by the public. He recommended the appointment of an Inspector General to carry out this role. This recommendation was accepted but the post did not sit easily within the bureaucratic machine of central government. The first and only holder of the post resigned from office before completing his second two-year term of office.

Lord Justice Woolf noted that there was a profound desire throughout the service for real leadership (para. 12.5) and recommended that this should be provided by a head who was seen to be in operational charge of the service (para. 12.29). Woolf went on to examine the relationship between government ministers and the prison service. He concluded that the prison service should become more clearly

> an operational organization which can be expected to work under the clear leadership of the Director General to the policies, priorities and with the resources established by Ministers (para. 12.44).

The government decided that from 1 April 1993 the prison services in England and Wales and in Scotland should become agencies, at one step removed from their parent government departments. One consequence of this change should be that the Directors of both services will be in a better position to offer the visible leadership advocated by Woolf within the context which he envisaged.

LESS CENTRALIZATION

The relationship between the central administrations of the prison services in the United Kingdom and staff in prisons has been problematic for many years. The headquarters organization is staffed mainly by administrative grade civil servants, very few of whom have any direct experience of prisons. Their craft is that of the generalist administrator. At the senior levels their work usually involves drafting policy and providing support for government ministers.

The prison service in England and Wales is a large executive organization with a turnover of around one and a half billion pounds each year and a staff of 40,000. The skills required to manage an organization of these dimensions are quite different from those traditionally demanded of administrators in the civil service.

Unlike other large social institutions, such as schools, hospitals, the police and probation service, the prison service is the only major civilian institution in our society which is directly under the executive control of central government. It is unique in that it takes care of a large number of men and women for 24 hours a day, 365 days a year, against their will. It attracts little notice when its affairs are going well but has a high potential for attracting unfavourable publicity when things go wrong. Because of the continual risk which it carries for political embarrassment it has been organized as a highly centralized bureaucracy. This attempt to exercise tight control by an administration which is not at ease with its executive function has led to a very dysfunctional organization.

Most successful organizations have what is described as a 'flat' structure. The function of a headquarters department is to set out policy, to define the objectives of the organization and to obtain resources to allow these objectives to be achieved. The implementation of policy and objectives should then be left to the executive parts of the organization. Headquarters should restrict itself to supporting these activities and to evaluating how well they are being implemented.

This was the model which Woolf recommended for the prison service.

> The role of Headquarters should be an enabling one: enabling Governors to govern and providing support for staff. This will involve a substantial change in the attitude of Headquarters (para. 1.179).

AN ENHANCED ROLE FOR PRISON OFFICERS

An absence of trust and of properly delegated authority is not just a feature of the relationship between those who work in prison headquarters and those who manage prisons. The most important set of relationships in any prison is that between the prisoner and the first-line prison officer. There is a very delicate balance between the coercive role of the prison officer, which has to ensure that prisoners are detained in as secure a form of custody as is necessary, and the caring role, which ensures that prisoners are treated with respect and given as much dignity as possible in their daily life.

One of the main tasks of management in a prison is to create a structure and a climate which enables such a balance to be maintained. Officers have to feel confident in exercising both the custodial and the caring aspects of their work. This will only happen if management shows that it trusts staff. Over the last 100 years the title of the first-line member of staff has changed from turnkey, to warder, to prison officer. It is not always clear that these changes of name have been marked by any real development of his or her role.

The last fifty years have seen an influx of new disciplines and professions in prisons: assistant governors, social workers, probation officers, teachers, psychiatrists, psychologists. All of them have concentrated on the 'caring' aspect of work with prisoners. Their relationship with prison officers has at times been difficult. Many of them have tended to look down on officers as mere custodians. Prison officers on the other hand have tended to dismiss them as people who work during office hours and who are not to be found when the going gets tough. In many instances officers have felt that they were being criticized for not being caring enough towards prisoners while at the same time other people were taking away the positive parts of their work.

A prison is an organic institution and needs to have contributions from many groups of people, each of which will have a different set of skills to offer. There is more than enough work for everyone. It remains true that the key staff are the prison officers. There are many more of them than any other group. Most of them will spend a professional lifetime in the prison service, many of them in the one prison. Other individuals and groups may come and go. The two groups which are continuously present in any prison are prisoners and prison officers.

The real atmosphere in any prison is determined by the relationship between prisoners and prison officers. If a new governor is to effect any change in a prison, he or she will achieve this, not by dealing directly with prisoners, but by the leadership and sense of direction which he or she gives to staff. Allowing staff to use their initiative and encouraging them to work positively with prisoners is quite simply good management practice.

It is important to have sound policies and clear leadership but Woolf had no doubt about the important role to be played by staff.

The quality of the prison system ultimately depends on the quality of the performance of the prison officers who have the day-to-day responsibility for dealing with prisoners (para. 1.180).

THE EXPECTATIONS OF THE PRISONER

Imprisonment presents the prisoner with an odd mixture of certainty and uncertainty. One of the greatest punishments of imprisonment is the grinding monotony of daily activity. The prisoner knows exactly what he or she will be doing tomorrow, next week, next month, next year and possibly for the next several years. Prison regime has very little challenge or variation. On the other hand there is the overpowering uncertainty which goes with not being in control of one's own activities. The prisoner may be transferred to another prison at short notice, may be moved from one work party to another, may or may not be selected for a course in education. Above all, the prisoner is likely to lose his or her place as a member of a family in all but name. Prisoners who are serving long sentences will be unsure of the date of their release from prison and will have to wait to hear of executive decisions which are made behind closed doors.

Being deprived of one's freedom is one of the greatest stresses a person is ever likely to face. This stress is compounded by the uncertainties which surround life in prison. In such a setting minor problems become magnified out of all proportion. It then may only take a spark to set off a violent reaction, either from an individual or from a group of prisoners.

Woolf recommended that a prisoner should have a clear sense of progress throughout the whole of his or her sentence. There should be an opportunity to serve a sentence in a constructive way, with the prisoner being given a series of choices which would encourage a greater sense of responsibility. Woolf suggested that the discussion which went on between prison staff and the prisoner in reaching agreement about how the time in prison could be put to best use should be expressed in the form of a compact which both parties to the agreement would be expected to honour.

SETTING STANDARDS

For people who spend their working lives within the prison system there is a real danger that the completely unacceptable becomes acceptable, or at least becomes unnoticed. In the dying years of the twentieth century in the United Kingdom, for example, there should not have been any need for a debate about when prisoners could expect to have continuous access to sanitation. When asked that question by the Public Accounts Committee in 1986 the Permanent Secretary at the Home Office replied, 'I do not know.'[18]

There are no standards laid down about how large prison cells should be, nor how much space a prisoner should be entitled to. The statutory prison rules simply say that prisoners should not be confined two to a cell which has been built to hold one person. Over the years this rule has been honoured in the breach. The prison service has no control over the number of people who are sent to prison. As this number increased, it became necessary to place two and sometimes three prisoners in a cell. But that is only an explanation as to why the statutory rule has been broken. It is not a justification for the breach. Prisoners are quite entitled to ask why they should be expected to obey all rules when the prison service itself can pick and choose which of its own rules it keeps.

The regime in most prisons extends into the smallest details of a prisoner's life. Depending on the prison in which he is held, he may have daily access to a shower or may only be able to shower once a week. He may be able to wear his own clothes or he may have to wear prison clothes. If it is the latter, the frequency with which underwear, shirts and socks are changed will vary from prison to prison. In some cases he will be allocated a personal set of clothes; in others his clothes will be given to him from a common stock each time they are laundered.

Meal times in many prisons seem to assume that the human stomach has the ability of a camel to store food until the body needs to digest it. It is not uncommon for the three main meals of the day to be served in an eight-hour period between 8.00 am and 4.00 pm, or over an even shorter period at weekends. That leaves sixteen hours between the main evening meal and breakfast the following morning.

Facilities for work, for training, for education, for courses which prepare a man or woman for release will vary enormously between prisons. They will normally be much better in prisons which hold prisoners serving long sentences than in local prisons. Even within similar types there will be significant differences.

For many years there has been pressure from groups within the prison service, such as the Prison Officers' Association and the Prison Governors' Association, and from reform groups and other external commentators to introduce a code of minimum standards which might be applied to all prisons. In 1983, in 1987 and again in 1990 Home Affairs Select Committees of the House of Commons supported this notion.

Despite an indication from the Home Secretary in 1982 that the Home Office was prepared to consider a code of minimum standards, the government was unwilling to commit itself to such a course of action. The argument against introducing a code of standards has usually been that any set of standards which reflected present reality would be so low as to be unacceptable. The converse of this argument has been that acceptable standards would be so unattainable as to be meaningless.

Woolf was not impressed by these and similar arguments (para. 12.07). He pointed out that there were precedents in the United Nations Standard Minimum Rules for the Treatment of Prisoners[19] and in the European Prison Rules.[20] He accepted the argument used by supporters of a set of minimum standards that they would be a benchmark against which the need for improvement could be measured.

Woolf recommended that the prison service should draw up and publish a set of what would be known as Accredited Standards. A timescale should then be set within which each standard could be reached in each prison. By the time the standards had been reached Woolf envisaged that they would be enshrined in a Prison Rule and be subject to judicial review.

OVERCROWDING

Unlike schools, hospitals and other large public institutions prisons are not able to put up 'house full' notices. The prison service, as the servant of the courts, cannot control the number of prisoners for which it has to care. Overcrowding has been the single most important obstacle to improving quality of service within many prisons, particularly the large local prisons in which the majority of the prison population is held.

There are several ways of dealing with this problem. The first is to accept without question that it is the responsibility of government to provide as many prison places as are needed for those whom the courts deprive of their liberty. This, by and large, is the route which has been followed in the United States of America. Between 1980 and 1990 the prison population in the United States rose from 500,000 to 1,250,000. This explosion has been matched by a massive increase in prison buildings, to the extent that in some states expenditure on new prisons is now the largest part of public capital spending. The problem with this strategy, as the United States authorities are discovering, is that the demand for prison spaces can become insatiable. Sir Alexander Paterson, the former English Prison Commissioner, remarked on this feature many years ago:

> Wherever prisons are built, Courts will make use of them. If no prison is handy, some other way of dealing with the offender will possibly be discovered. [21]

In some countries a ceiling is put on the number of people held in prison at any one time without interfering with the absolute right of courts to sentence people to imprisonment. One way of doing this, as in the Netherlands, is by requiring offenders who do not pose an immediate danger to the public to wait after sentence until a prison space becomes available for them to serve their sentence. Another possibility, as happens in some Canadian provincial systems, is to release prisoners who are coming to the end of their sentences in order to ensure that a prison never holds more prisoners than it has accommodation for.

Woolf recognized how important it is for the stability of any prison that it should not be required to hold more prisoners than it can cope with. He recommended that a new Prison Rule should be introduced to the effect that no prison would hold more prisoners than it had certified accommodation for. If any prison had to exceed its certified accommodation for more than seven days in any three months, the Home Secretary would be required to issue a certificate specifying the level of overcrowding which was permitted and the reasons for it. Such a certificate would be valid for up to three months and would have to be laid before both Houses of Parliament. In the event, this was one of the few recommendations in the report which the Home Secretary was not prepared to accept.

Woolf was aware that there would be little point in making any recommendation about the level of the prison population without considering the reasons why people are sent to prison. His terms of reference excluded him from considering sentencing policy directly. However, he did comment extensively on the nature of the prison population.

He started from the premise that 'only those for whom prison is essential should be there' (para. 1.204.). The statutory basis of this position was confirmed in section 1(2)of the Criminal Justice Act 1991. In respect of those prisoners who are in prison awaiting trial, Woolf was quite explicit:

> (There are) a substantial number of people remanded
> in custody who should not be in prison (para. 10.79).

He urged more active cooperation among the courts, the prosecution service, the probation service and the prison service to reduce the number of people remanded in custody and to limit the periods of time spent on remand. Some people who are charged with offences require some limit to be placed on their freedom of movement which falls far short of incarceration behind the high walls of a prison. For many of these a condition of residence in their own home, sometimes linked with a requirement to report to the local police, is sufficient. Others might have to be required to live in a bail hostel, which is much less secure and much less expensive than a prison, but still with sufficient restriction on liberty. It is essential that the courts have sufficient information to allow them to reach an informed decision about what restrictions need to be placed on an accused person's freedom of movement.

It is still possible in the United Kingdom that a person who is fined by the court but who either cannot or will not pay that fine will end up in prison. The court has considered all the facts of the case and has decided that imprisonment is inappropriate. Nonetheless, the person ends up in prison. Such an outcome threatens the credibility of the criminal justice system.

The Criminal Justice Act 1991 introduced the practice of unit fines into England and Wales. This arrangement, which already exists in several other countries, related the size of the fine to an offender's disposable income. Woolf recommended that once this new arrangement had bedded down consideration should be given to removing the threat of imprisonment for non-payment of fine and replacing this with some form of civil action (para. 10.113). In 1993 the Criminal Justice Act 1991 was amended and the provision for unit fines was removed.

Particular care has to be taken when it is necessary to deprive young people of their liberty. Woolf was especially concerned at the imprisonment of young men and women under the age of 17 years (para. 10.107). This matter was also dealt with in the Criminal Justice Act 1991.[22]

The number of mentally disordered people held in prisons in England and Wales has regularly attracted public criticism. Mental health legislation has proved singularly ineffective in ensuring that offenders who are mentally ill are referred to health services rather than into the criminal justice system. Woolf noted that attempts were being made to deal with this problem by the introduction of various diversion systems. Despite this Woolf was forced to conclude:

> It is, however, clear that there will remain for the foreseeable future, a significant problem for the Prison Service in accommodating mentally disordered offenders (para. 10.136).

Woolf urged the prison service to make special provision for them and for prisoners with mental handicap.

ACCESS TO SANITATION

Rule 12 of the United Nations Standard Minimum Rules for the Treatment of Prisoners provides:

> The sanitary installations shall be adequate to enable every prisoner to comply with the needs of nature when necessary and in a clean and decent manner.[23]

The daily spectacle of long lines of men trudging to sluice sinks carrying slopping, foetid chamber pots has become a symbol of the worst aspects of the prison systems in the United Kingdom. These sad morning processions begin in many prisons as soon as prisoners are unlocked after twelve or more hours confined, sometimes alongside one or two other people, in small cells with no access to proper sanitary facilities.

Woolf described this lack of sanitation as the most destructive feature of the prison system after overcrowding.

> It destroys the morale of prisoners and staff. It is uncivilized and a symptom of an archaic prison system (para. 1.192).

The prison service had stated that it gave a high priority to ensuring that prisoners had continuous access to proper sanitation, but no timetable had been set. Woolf recommended that a public commitment should be given to achieve this by February 1996, a date which had been recommended in 1989 by the Chief Inspector of Prisons.

In the course of responding on 25 February 1991 to the publication of the Woolf Report the Home Secretary indicated that the prison service could and should do better than meet the target set in the report. He undertook that all prisoners would have access to sanitation day and night by the end of 1994.

It is a sad reflection on the state of English prisons that an undertaking to provide such a basic human right had to be given at the end of the twentieth century. There should be as little delay as possible in making the necessary provision. However, the decision to provide full access to sanitation within such a tight timetable has meant that other much needed improvements have been given a lower priority in the short term. Interestingly, a recent survey of prisoners[24] has shown that they have a somewhat different set of priorities. Continuous access to a toilet came after a wish for better food, for more frequent visits and for access to pay telephones.

LINKS WITH THE OUTSIDE WORLD

Men and women who are deprived of their liberty have a right to be treated decently while they are in prison. It is equally important that they should be given the opportunity to maintain and to develop links with their families and with friends. They should also be encouraged to understand that they are members of a wider society, to which they can contribute and from which they can benefit.

Until now prisons have been regarded primarily as places of exile to which people who have broken, or are thought to have broken, certain rules of society are sent. The notion of any real contact with the rest of society during this period of exile has been discouraged. Almost reluctantly, prisoners have been allowed to maintain limited contact with their immediate families, although this too has been made difficult. Prisoners are very often held in prisons which are far from home. This is an added hardship for partners, children and other friends who have to travel long and arduous journeys to visit. Correspondence by letter has been restricted, both in respect of the number and length of letters which may be sent and received and because letters have been subject to routine censorship.

This concept of the prison as a place of exile has had several negative consequences. It has led men and women who are in prison to regard the experience of imprisonment as something which is divorced from and which bears no relevance to the real world. Very often the normal rules of society do not apply in prison. Behaviour which would be unthinkable in everyday life somehow becomes acceptable.

It is an odd system which sends people to prison in the hope that they will become more responsible yet which, the moment they step through the prison gate, takes all responsibility from them. Prisoners are left with little responsibility for any of the details of their own life. The state will often take over responsibility for the support of their families. And at the end of a sentence of imprisonment, the prisoner is expected to feel a greater sense of responsibility.

In an environment which is cut off from everyday outside influences, prisoners are unlikely to feel any sense of commitment to society or to have any stake in the community from which they have come and to which they will one day return. Small wonder that recidivism rates among former prisoners remain as high as they do.

Woolf recognized the implications of this way of treating prisoners.

> The evidence before the Inquiry suggests that at least part of the explanation for imprisonment not being more successful in preventing reoffending is that the prisoner has so little responsibility for what happens to him during the period of the sentence (para. 10.27).

His solution was that the artificial barriers which separate the experience of imprisonment from the reality of everyday living should be demolished so that 'life in prison will be as close to life outside as the demands of imprisonment permit'.

One of the most important priorities for prisoners is the need to keep in contact with their families. This can be done in several ways. There should be no reason to place any restriction on the frequency or amount of correspondence which prisoners may have with their families. Correspondence should only be scrutinized when there is a genuine threat to the security of the establishment or in the interests of justice. There is likely to be no need for this in medium or minimum security establishments. In secure prisons there may be a need to open incoming mail to ensure that it does not contain weapons, money or other items which might present a threat to others. If possible, this should be done in the presence of the recipient. The only correspondence which should be read is that to and from prisoners in the highest security category, where there is a clear threat to the security of the public.

Almost all prisoners in United Kingdom prisons now have access to pay telephones. These allow them to make but not to receive calls. Prisoners place this form of immediate access to family and friends high on their list of priorities.

Face-to-face contact is particularly important for any human relationship. In most prisons this will take place in special visiting rooms. These vary greatly in terms of the quality of visit which is possible. In many cases visits take place in a large barn of a room where there is little privacy. The furniture in some rooms will consist of long rows of tables which are no more than shelves, with prisoners seated on one side and visitors on the other. In other prisons there will be small tables around which the prisoner and visitors can sit. Some prisons will have refreshment facilities and a creche for small children.

No matter what efforts are made to improve the environment of such visiting rooms it remains very difficult to maintain close links with one's family in such a setting, particularly over a long number of years. One of the first priorities of any prison system should be to reduce the pressure which deprivation of liberty places on a family unit. The best way of doing this is to allow prisoners to go home regularly for short periods of time. This practice reminds prisoners of their place in the family and reduces the pain of imprisonment for other members of the family. It makes the prisoner more conscious of the reality of being deprived of liberty while at the same time preparing for what is likely to happen on eventual release.

In many countries prisoners are given such leave once or twice a year shortly after beginning even relatively long sentences. It is easier to prevent a relationship breaking down than to put it together again after a break of many years. The decision to allow prisoners to go home on leave has to be made after an assessment as to the possibility that they might not return and the threat to the public if they do not. The reality is that the vast majority of prisoners do return to prison at the end of their leave period. The prospect of future leave is too important to be placed in jeopardy.

There will inevitably be a small number of prisoners who present too great a threat to the public or to other individuals to be allowed home. In several prison systems provision is made for loved ones to spend longer periods in prison. Some prisons in North America, for example, have mobile homes sited discreetly within the secure perimeter where prisoners are allowed to spend two or three days in privacy with their families once or twice a year. Very often the visitor will be a spouse or partner. Frequently children will come; on occasion the visitors will be parents, sisters or brothers. For this short period the group is able to live as a family. The likelihood that the prisoner will eventually be able to return to the family as a full member is increased. This is one of main objectives of these arrangements:

> The Private Family Visiting Program was created for
> the purpose of assisting in the maintenance of family
> ties in order to promote re-integration of the offender
> into the community upon his or her release. [25]

These arrangements are more humane than those to be found, for example, in some Scandinavian countries. There many prisons have private rooms to which prisoners and their partners may retire for a period of two or three hours. The whole process is very clinical and somewhat demeaning to both parties, particularly the one who has to visit.

Family visits have not yet been introduced in any of the prison systems in the United Kingdom although the Scottish prison service gave an undertaking in 1990 to consider the possibility of doing so.[26]

If maintaining contact with the world outside the prison is to be important, it is logical that prisoners should be held in prisons which are reasonably close to the communities from which they have come and to which they will return on release. Woolf was quite specific on this point:

> . . . prisons should be community prisons sited within reasonable proximity to, and having close connections with, the community with which the prisoners they hold have their closest links (para. 11.49).

Since publication of the Woolf Report there has been some discussion within the prison service in England and Wales about the concept of community prisons. There has been debate about whether some prisons should be identified as 'community prisons' on an experimental basis. This discussion betrays a misunderstanding of what Woolf had in mind. This was simply a recognition of the best practice which already existed.

> We therefore recommend that the Prison Service should adopt a policy objective of accommodating the majority of prisoners in community prisons. Local prisons already largely conform to this policy (para. 11.62).

This involves an acceptance of the principle that prisons do not exist in isolation. They exist because the community wants them to exist and they operate on behalf of the community. The community has a right to know what goes on behind their high walls and also has an obligation to be involved in their activities. To use a current phrase, the walls of the prison should be 'permeable'; that is, prisoners should be encouraged to become involved in the activities of the community and the community should take part in many of the activities of the prison.

This two-way process works to the benefit of all those involved. There is a great deal of unused talent in every prison. Prisoners respond well to the suggestion that they might have something to contribute to people who are more disadvantaged than themselves. This help might take the form of groups of people from the community, particularly the old, the young and the handicapped, coming into prisons to make use of their facilities or to be looked after by prisoners. It might take the form of selected prisoners going out into the community to help similar groups.

It might also mean that instead of trying to operate as a total institution, duplicating many resources which already exist in the community, prisons might make use of the facilities which already exist in the community such as health care, education and skills training.

Woolf pointed out that close links between a prison and its local community could have other benefits. It makes sense, for example, that prisons should be close to the courts which they serve. There are also advantages if prison staff come from the same area as the prisoners in their care (para. 11.55). A visitor to Attica Prison in the United States of America is immediately struck by the fact that the majority of prisoners are black urban males from New York City while the majority of guards come from white farming stock in upstate New York. Culturally the two groups are quite distinct. There are several similar examples in the United Kingdom: staff from the West Country of England who look after London prisoners in Dartmoor; staff from the farming and fishing communities of the northeast of Scotland who look after prisoners from Glasgow and Edinburgh in Peterhead. Whatever the good will, it is difficult for two diverse groups like these not to feel alienated from each other in a prison setting.

Woolf recognized that it would be difficult in some prisons which are in isolated locations to develop close links between prisoners and the local community. He recommended that in these situations prisons should group together to form a community cluster. He also recommended women and young prisoners might be held in separate facilities within large local prisons to give them the benefit of these community links.

SMALL UNITS IN PRISONS

The first thing which imprisonment does to a person is to strip away the features of individuality. Prisoners can expect to be dressed in prison uniform and to be given a number. The typical prison holds a specified number of human beings who are deprived of their liberty for a variety of different reasons. It holds a homogeneous group of 'prisoners'. This one feature which unites them is more important than the thousand and one differences which separate them as persons. Or at least, that is the conventional wisdom.

The anonymity which is common to most prisons is exaggerated the greater the number of prisoners it holds. It is possible for a man or woman held in an establishment of 300 or 400 people to retain a degree of individuality in the eyes of those who manage the prison. All semblance of individuality disappears in a prison which holds 3, 4 or 5,000 prisoners. The anonymity in these cases will probably extend to the staff who look after the prisoners. They will not be known to each other or to senior management.

With this anonymity comes an absence of any sense of personal responsibility and of any meaningful relationship between groups of people. Prisoners are regarded, often by themselves and certainly by others, as a type. The same applies to prison staff. The person will then respond to given situations according to type, rather than as an individual.

This culture, which applies to many kinds of large institution, can result in organizations failing to recognize the needs of the individual. It can also lead to individuals becoming involved in kinds of behaviour which they would normally avoid. It is no coincidence that some of the worst prison riots have occurred in very large prisons, often holding numbers of prisoners far in excess of their capacity. When the riot broke out in Strangeways Prison in Manchester on 1 April 1990 the prison had space for 970 prisoners. It was holding 1647.

Woolf began his discussion of the nature of prison buildings by expressing a clear and definite opinion:

> The first principle is that normally prisoners should be accommodated in prison units of approximately 50/70

prisoners. The prison itself should not hold more than
400 prisoners, though when this is necessary there can
be more than one discrete prison within a larger prison
(para. 11.7).

Following his inquiry into the riot at Manchester Woolf made this
recommendation on the grounds of security and control. He
wanted to prevent a situation arising again in which an incident
could begin in one part of a prison and spread quickly throughout
the whole prison. But this was not merely a matter of physical
control.

The security and management advantages of small
units should result in a greater feeling of security for
prisoners and for prison staff. They should therefore
result in improved relations and in better justice for
prisoners (para. 1.202).

Most large prisons have been designed to take account of the penal
philosophy of the nineteenth century. This was based on the
principle that prisoners should be confined in individual cells
where they could contemplate the error of their past ways. They
had very little contact with each other. Buildings which were
designed for this form of imprisonment are largely inappropriate
for the penal philosophy of the late twentieth century which
advocates the need for prisoners to enjoy as active a regime as
possible, while also being given the opportunity to face up to
personal problems.

The manner in which some prison systems have dealt with
prisoners who cannot or will not live among the general run of
prisoners provides a useful model. These may be prisoners who
require to be kept apart for their own safety, for example, because
of the nature of their crime or because they have fallen foul of other
prisoners for a variety of reasons. They may be prisoners who have
had difficulty in settling to their sentences and who are disruptive
in one way or another.

The general principle for managing these prisoners is a simple
one. It involves bringing them together in small groups to be looked
after by dedicated groups of staff. Originally the decision to go
down this road was prompted by the need to segregate these

prisoners for reasons of good order or security. It also provided an alternative to locking up such prisoners in isolation cells for long periods of time.

This system of managing prisoners in small groups allowed staff and prisoners for the first time to view each other as individuals. It also created a sense of community among the group who were required to live and work together for long periods of time. The best examples of this way of working are to be found in Butner Federal Correctional Institution in the United States, Grendon Underwood Prison in England and the Barlinnie Special Unit in Scotland.

This principle of restricting the size of groups of prisoners to an extent which allowed individual strengths and weaknesses to be taken into account and which also allowed some notion of community accountability need not be restricted to particular groups of prisoners. If it is more widely applied it may make life more safe and more purposeful for the majority of prisoners.

Victorian prisons are not ideally suited to this style of living. It would be better to have prisons which are specifically designed for regimes of this type. In 1984 the Home Office Control Review Committee described the potential of what were known as 'new generation' prisons in the United States of America.[27] These were based on the concept of separate units which would hold between 50 and 100 prisoners. They contained not only cells but also all the facilities which were needed for a constructive existence.

It should be axiomatic that the design of prisons, like those of any other institution, should be based on the philosophy on which the management of these establishments is based. In 1984 and 1985 members of a Home Office Working Group visited several of these new prisons in the United States.[28] They concluded that this new concept in design did indicate a move away from the notion that prisoners should be 'treated' while in prison to one in which prisoners would be held in safe and humane establishments where they would be given opportunities and encouraged to change their own behaviour.

Central to this concept was a decentralized management system. As much authority as possible was delegated to the staff who were directly responsible for the prisoners. In its report the Control Review Committee commented on the outcome of this way of running a prison:

Decentralized unit management is claimed to increase contact between staff and inmates, foster better interpersonal relationships, and lead to more knowledgeable decision-making as a direct result of staff dealing with smaller, more permanent groups of inmates (para. 18).

These principles can best be applied in prisons which have been designed for this purpose. It is also possible, although more complicated, to apply them in more traditional prisons by a process of managing individual accommodation blocks separately and further dividing their management. These are the principles which were recommended to Woolf and which he in turn took up in his report (para. 11.11).

REMAND PRISONERS

When a person is charged with committing a criminal offence the presumption should always be that such an individual will remain in society until such time as he or she is brought to trial. This does happen in the vast majority of cases in the United Kingdom. Sometimes it is necessary to place some condition on the continuing freedom of an accused person but this normally falls far short of complete deprivation of liberty. The Woolf Report cites the assertion of the Minister of State at the Home Office, speaking in September 1989, that

> . . . people should be remanded in custody only when this is absolutely necessary and for the shortest possible time (para. 10.76).

The courts do remand a significant minority of accused people in prison to await trial. Approximately 20 per cent of those who are in prison in the United Kingdom are awaiting trial; that is, they have yet to be found guilty of the offence with which they are charged. Many of them will eventually be found not guilty or will receive a non-custodial sentence. In 1990 60 per cent of male defendants who had been remanded in custody and 77 per cent of female defendants, 61 per cent of all defendants, came into this category.

Given the fact that unconvicted prisoners are innocent in law they should not be treated as if they had been already found guilty and sentenced to a period of imprisonment. Every effort should be made to enable them to keep as much contact as possible with their families. They should be given every opportunity to consult with their lawyers and to prepare their defence. They should not be subjected to the same regime as convicted prisoners.

The reality which Woolf found is that prisoners on remand 'unjustly suffer some of the worst conditions in the prison system' (para. 1.204). The prison service has to allocate its resources sparingly. Traditionally the greatest proportion of resources, both in terms of accommodation and of facilities goes to those prisoners who are serving long sentences. This is explained on the basis that these men and women are in prison for the longest periods and are most likely to benefit from such facilities as better work and education opportunities. It may also be that they are most likely to complain if they are given poor facilities.

Local prisons, which hold convicted prisoners serving short sentences and remand prisoners, fare worst when resources are allocated. Within local prisons, those who are unconvicted fare worst of all. The arguments which are frequently used are that remand prisoners have to concentrate on preparing their defence, that since they cannot be obliged to work there will be uncertainty from day to day as to whether they will be prepared to and, anyway, they are likely to spend a proportion of each day being visited by family or friends or in consultation with their lawyers. And, so the argument goes, unconvicted prisoners are only in prison for a very short period. The reality is that many unconvicted prisoners serve several months in prison and for much of that time have very little to do.

The prison service has a statement of purpose, which is a brief description of how it aims to treat convicted prisoners. Woolf urged that a separate statement of purpose was needed setting out the responsibilities of the prison service in respect of remand prisoners. He also recommended that the presumption should be that prisoners on remand should be treated as security category C rather than, as at present, category B. This would open up many more opportunities for constructive activities.

STANDARDS OF JUSTICE

It is fundamental that prison systems should be administered in a manner which is fair and just and which is seen to be so. In the coercive environment of a prison it is imperative that there should be a clearly defined set of procedures which allows a prisoner to make a request or complaint or to air a grievance and to have confidence that the matter will be considered fairly and objectively. These procedures must be drawn up in such a way that they can be understood and accepted both by prisoners and by those who are responsible for the administration of prisons. In addition to the principles of fairness and justice, it is in the interests of all concerned that these procedures should embody certain characteristics such as speed, efficiency, accessibility, credibility, reasonableness, objectivity, flexibility and sensitivity.

In 1982 Lord Wilberforce ruled that

> in spite of his imprisonment, a convicted prisoner retains all civil rights which are not taken away expressly or by necessary implication.[29]

In respect of remedies for violations of human rights, the International Covenant on Civil and Political Rights[30] provides that:

> 2. Each State Party to the present Covenant undertakes:
>
> a. to ensure that any person whose rights or freedoms as herein recognized are violated shall have an effective remedy, notwithstanding that the violation has been committed by persons acting in an official capacity;
>
> b. to ensure that any person claiming such a remedy shall have his right thereto determined by competent judicial, administrative or legislative authorities, or by any other competent authority provided for by the legal system of the State, and to develop the possibilities of judicial remedy;
>
> c. to ensure that the competent authority shall enforce such remedies when granted.

There can be no justification for the actions of the prisoners who rioted at Strangeways in April 1990. However, it is clear that many of them felt that legitimate avenues of complaint had been closed to them. They were of the opinion, however erroneously, that their complaints would only be listened to if they took violent action (Woolf, para. 14.298). They were not the first prisoners to act in this way. The history of the prison services in the United Kingdom over the last twenty years is littered with examples of violent protest by prisoners, from Peterhead to Parkhurst. A similar story can be told worldwide, from the United States to Chile, from France to Australia.

Woolf drew a simple conclusion with regard to these matters:

> There must also be justice in our prisons. The system of justice which has put a person in prison cannot end at the prison doors. It must accompany the prisoner into the prison, his cell, and to all aspects of his life in prison (para. 14.19).

Any proper system of remedies must guarantee prisoners

> natural justice, respect, access to information, the right to express their case, assistance with representation, a statement of reasons for any decision, no undue delay, an indication of available remedies and independent scrutiny.

The resolution of any request or complaint which a prisoner may have should be achieved as close as possible to the source of the matter at issue. Prisoners should have direct access to people who make decisions about them and should be able to discuss the reasons why decisions are made. This is an argument for delegating responsibility for decision-making in prisons to the lowest appropriate level.

Even within a preventive culture, it will not always be possible to resolve issues at a first level. If a prisoner feels that he or she has a legitimate complaint, there should be a possibility of appeal first to the governor of the prison and, if that still fails to resolve the matter, to prison service headquarters. These rights are provided for in the United Nations Standard Minimum Rule 36.

Prisoners should also be able to raise complaints externally. Prisoners are members of society who are being subjected to specific sanctions. When they feel that the prison system is failing to meet its obligations they should have unhindered access to independent consideration of their complaints. This can take several forms.

If a prisoner alleges that either members of staff or other prisoners have committed an act, such as an assault, which contravenes the criminal law, the prisoner should have confidential access to the police or prosecuting authorities. Prisoners should also be able to seek legal advice about any matter which affects their treatment in prison. They should also be free to raise issues with any other individual or group whom they think might help them to resolve a problem.

Each prison in England and Wales has a Board of Visitors. The equivalent in Scotland is the Visiting Committee. These Boards are made up of independent members who are appointed by the Home Secretary. They have no executive function. Their main function, endorsed by Woolf, is as 'watchdogs for the Home Secretary'. One way of carrying out this function is by taking up individual complaints which are made to them by prisoners.

Despite all these provisions, Woolf was quite clear about the need for a truly independent element in any grievance procedure for prisoners:

> The case for some form of independent person or body to consider grievances is incontrovertible. There is no possibility of the present system satisfactorily meeting this point, even once it has bedded down. A system without an independent element is not a system which accords with proper standards of justice (para. 14.345).

Woolf recommended that a Complaints Adjudicator should be appointed and should have two distinct roles. He or she should 'recommend, advise and conciliate' at the final stage of the grievance procedure and should also act as a final tribunal of appeal in disciplinary proceedings. In one important respect Woolf's recommendation fell short of the standard required in international instruments as regards independence. The powers of the Adjudicator were to be restricted to recommending and did not include any power of implementation.

Prisons should be safe environments for all who live and work in them, that is, for the prisoners and for the staff. No one in a prison should fear for his or her physical safety. It is the responsibility of prison authorities to ensure that this is the case. This means that there must be good order in a prison. Good order is best achieved by positive means. Prisoners would prefer not to be in prison but most will accept the fact that they are there. If they are kept occupied and given the opportunity to use their time positively they will respond to the reasonable rules and regulations which are necessary in any large group of people to ensure that good order is maintained.

But from time to time prisoners will refuse to observe rules which have been reasonably imposed. When this happens there has to be a formal disciplinary procedure. In the prison service in England and Wales 22 offences against discipline are listed in Prison Rule 47 as amended by the Prison (Amendment) Rules 1989. The punishments which may be awarded for any of these offences are also listed in the rules. The procedures to be followed in terms of advising a prisoner that he or she is to be charged with a disciplinary offence, of laying the charge and of the hearing itself are defined in detail.

In addition to being a form of public watchdog of what goes on in a prison the Board of Visitors at the time of the Woolf Report acted as a higher tribunal to which the governor could refer disciplinary charges which, if proved, would merit a more severe punishment than was available to him or her. The governor, for example, has powers to punish a prisoner by loss of up to 28 days' remission. The Board of Visitors had the power to punish with up to 120 days' loss of remission. Woolf pointed out (para. 14.385) that this was equivalent to a prison sentence of nine months, allowing that prisoners were entitled to one third remission. This sentence is greater than is available in a Magistrates' Court.

The important point is that neither the hearing carried out by the governor in what is known as the orderly room, nor the hearing previously held by the Board of Visitors, is a court of law. They are administrative procedures. If a criminal act is committed in a prison, it should be dealt with in the same manner as a criminal act committed in the community. That is, it should be investigated by the police and a decision should be made by the Crown Prosecution Service about whether charges should be pursued in a court of law. The internal disciplinary system should deal only with breaches of prison discipline and with minor criminal matters which would not usually merit any response from the police.

Woolf was quite clear as to what was required:

> If penalties equivalent to quite long prison sentences are required, then it is more satisfactory that they should be awarded by a Court. That would allow a trial which provides the full safeguards of the criminal law (para. 14.402).

He recommended that Boards of Visitors should be relieved of their powers of adjudication in order to allow them to concentrate on their watchdog role. Governors should deal with all breaches of discipline within their existing powers and alleged criminal acts committed in prison should be subjected to the normal process of the criminal law.

THE RESPONSE TO THE WOOLF REPORT

The Woolf Report contains the twelve main recommendations which have been described above in some detail. It also makes 204 proposals. It is a seminal document which towers above previous inquiries into the prison system. This is not simply because of its wide-ranging set of proposals and recommendations, nor because of the open way in which Lord Justice Woolf went about his inquiry, important as both of these features are. It is because for the first time an official inquiry exposed the bedrock on which any prison system has to be based.

In the first place, it has to be *just*. People are sent to prison by a court of justice. One of the reasons for sending them to prison is the hope that they will be encouraged to live in a law abiding manner when they are released. If this is to be more than a pious hope, they must learn a respect for justice while they are in prison. This is only likely to occur if they are themselves treated justly. It is also important that people who work in the prison system operate within a context of justice and use it as a benchmark for all they do.

Secondly, prisons must not exist in isolation. They must reinforce their links with the community in which they exist.

Prisoners come from a community and will return to a community on release. Their alienation from the community will have begun before they committed the crime for which they were sent to prison. It is important that this alienation should not be reinforced while they are in prison. If the experience of imprisonment is to be at all rehabilitative, prisoners must be given some sense of belonging to a community while they are in prison and having something to contribute to that community to which they will one day return.

The government's considered response to the Woolf Report was contained in the White Paper 'Custody, Care and Justice'.[31] The government had already accepted the vast majority of Woolf's recommendations. The White Paper described how the recommendations would be implemented. It is a positive document which was warmly welcomed. The main concern expressed by several commentators was that no timetable was given for the programme of implementation and that as a consequence the most radical aspects of the report would quietly be shelved. It remains to be seen whether these fears will be realized.

REFERENCES

1. Report of an Inquiry into Prison Disturbances April 1990 (1991) (Woolf Report), Cmnd 1456, HMSO, London, para. 3.131.
2. Committee of Inquiry into the United Kingdom Prison Services (1979), Cmnd 7673, HMSO, London, para. 1.1.
3. Report of the Departmental Committee on Prisons (1895), Cmnd 7702, HMSO, London.
4. Report of the Departmental Committee Appointed to Inquire into the Pay and Conditions of Service at the Borstal and Prison Institutions in England and Scotland and at Broadmoor Criminal Lunatic Asylum (1923), Cmnd 1959, HMSO, London.
5. Report on the Circumstances Connected with the Recent Disorder at Dartmoor Convict Prison (1932), Cmnd 4010, HMSO, London.
6. Thomas, J E (1972), *The English Prison Officer Since 1850*, Routledge & Kegan Paul, London, p. 162.
7. Report of the Committee on Remunerations and Conditions of Service of Certain Grades in the Prison Services (1958), Cmnd 544, HMSO, London.
8. Thomas, J E (1972), *The English Prison Officer Since 1850*, Routledge & Kegan Paul, London, p. 210.
9. Report of the Inquiry into Prison Escapes and Security (1966), Cmnd 3175, HMSO, London.

10. Report of the Advisory Council on the Penal System on the Regime for Long Term Prisoners in Conditions of Maximum Security (1968), HMSO, London.
11. Report of the Committee of Inquiry into the United Kingdom Prison Services (1979), Cmnd 7673, HMSO, London.
12. Prison Reform Trust (1991), 'The Woolf Report', PRT, London.
13. House of Commons, Hansard vol. 170, col. 1342, 5 April 1990.
14. Morgan, R (1991), 'Woolf: In Retrospect and Prospect', *The Modern Law Review*, vol. 54:5, p. 722.
15. Morgan, R (1991), 'Woolf: In Retrospect and Prospect', *The Modern Law Review*, vol. 54:5, p. 722.
16. This arrangement was not acceptable to the Scottish Office, which took the view that it would be invidious for members of the Scottish Prison Service to speculate on how the prison service might be run in England and Wales. For this reason, the author was unable to accept Lord Woolf's invitation to take part in the seminars.
17. Criminal Justice Act 1991, Section 1(2).
18. Minutes of Evidence taken before the Public Accounts Committee, Session 1985-1986, 17 February 1986, Q 1285, HMSO.
19. UN Standard Minimum Rules for the Treatment of Prisoners, adopted by the First United Nations Congress on the Prevention of Crime and the Treatment of Offenders, held at Geneva in 1955, and approved by the Economic and Social Council by its resolutions 663 C (XXIV) of 31 July 1957 and 2076 (LXII) of 13 May 1977.
20. Council of Europe Standard Minimum Rules for the Treatment of Prisoners, Resolution (73) 5 of the Committee of Ministers of the Council of Europe.
21. Ruck, S K ed (1951), *Paterson on Prisons: Being the Collected Papers of Sir Alexander Paterson,* Muller, London.
22. NACRO, Criminal Justice Act 1991, Defendants and Offenders Under 18, NACRO, London.
23. United Nations Standard Minimum Rules for the Treatment of Prisoners adopted by the First UN Congress on the Prevention of Crime and the Treatment of Offenders, 1955, and approved by the Economic and Social Council in 1957 and 1977.
24. Office of Population Censuses and Surveys (1992), The National Prison Survey 1991, HMSO, London.
25. Evaluation of the Family Visiting Program (1988), Corporate Policy and Planning Division, Correctional Service of Canada, Ottawa.
26. 'Opportunity and Responsibility: Developing New Approaches to the Management of the Long-term Prison System in Scotland' (1990), Scottish Prison Service, Edinburgh.
27. Home Office (1984), 'Managing the Long-term Prison System', The Report of the Control Review Committee, HMSO, London.
28. Home Office (1985),'New Directions in Prison Design', Report of a Home Office Study of New Generation Prisons in the USA, HMSO, London.

29. Raymond v Honey (1983) 1 A.C.1, p. 10.
30. International Covenant on Civil and Political Rights, adopted by the General Assembly of the United Nations, 16 December 1966; entered into force 23 March 1976.
31. Home Office (1991),'Custody, Care and Justice: The Way Ahead for the Prison Service in England and Wales', HMSO, London.

ELEVEN

The Prison Service Machine

THE DEVELOPMENT OF THE BUREAUCRACY

Extensive use of imprisonment as a direct sentence of the court has become common only in the last few hundred years. Before that time the principal sentences available to courts were exile, often in the form of transportation, and execution. In many jurisdictions corporal punishment was quite common. Monetary penalties, which remain today the most common punishment imposed by courts in many countries, were very common. Prisons were used primarily as places in which to hold people who were awaiting trial or payment of a fine or debt or execution of another sentence such as the death penalty or exile. Imprisonment as a direct punishment appears to have been more common in England[1] than in other countries such as Scotland,[2] but even there it was not used as a matter of course.

The prisons which existed were generally managed by such people as sheriffs or justices of the peace who were responsible for maintaining law and order in the community. Offenders would be committed to these prisons by the local courts. Gradually the upkeep and management of the prisons became the responsibility of local authorities, such as county and town councils. They were usually administered by a committee of magistrates. Thus, the link between the court and the prison was recognized to be an important one.

Throughout the last years of the eighteenth and the early years of the nineteenth century, the general state of the prisons in the United Kingdom led to continuous criticism from a succession of public-spirited individuals, the best known of whom was John Howard whose report on *The State of the Prisons in England and Wales* [3] was particularly influential. The most significant response from the government to these growing expressions of concern was the introduction of the Prisons Act of 1835. This recognized that central government could no longer leave the oversight of prisons entirely in the hands of the various local authorities. The Act gave the Secretary of State the power to appoint up to five individuals to visit and inspect every gaol, bridewell, house of correction, penitentiary, prison or other place of confinement of prisoners in Great Britain and to examine any person holding office in such an establishment, to inspect all books and papers relating thereto and to inquire into all relevant matters. The inspectors were to make separate reports in writing, all of which were to be presented to Parliament.

During the following forty or so years successive Inspectors of Prisons led the drive for an improvement in conditions and in the administration of prisons. In a progressive way central government set the standards which were expected and local authorities were required to meet them. The inspectors took a broad definition of their role. They frequently demanded that changes be made in arrangements in individual prisons. In 1843 a code of rules for general application was published by the government.

Until the middle of the eighteenth century the direct involvement of central government in the United Kingdom in the care of men and women convicted by courts was restricted to those sentenced to transportation, which was widely used by courts in England. As the use of transportation became less frequent, an alternative form of punishment was required. In 1810 the House of Commons set up a select committee to consider the need for national penitentiaries. [4] Following publication of the committee's report, the government decided to go ahead with building a national penitentiary. Millbank Penitentiary, built on the site of what is now the Tate Gallery, admitted its first prisoners in 1816. The short and uninspiring history of this prison has been recorded by McConville. [5]

The principle of national penitentiaries was extended. Pentonville and Perth Prisons were opened in 1842 and a penitentiary for juveniles was opened at Parkhurst on the Isle of Wight. Two years later the government appointed Captain Joshua Jebb of the Royal Engineers as its first Surveyor General of Prisons. The importance of this post went beyond the technical advice which had first been sought. As well as having increasing authority in the administration of the new government prisons, Jebb was frequently consulted by local authorities in matters to do with the prisons for which they were responsible.

The expansion of a central prison administration continued with the establishment in 1850 of the Directorate of Convict Prisons to oversee the administration of all central prisons. Lieutenant Colonel Jebb was appointed its first chairman.

The management of all prisons in England and Wales was taken over by central government with the passing of the Prisons Act of 1877. This centralizing legislation was the result not so much of political ideology nor of philosophical dogma as of pragmatism. The Conservative government of Disraeli was not in favour of centralizing legislation but came under great pressure to restore the balance between local and central taxation. Transferring the cost of the prison system from the ratepayer to the taxpayer was one way of achieving this.

Captain, later Sir, Edmund du Cane of the Royal Engineers had been chairman of the Directorate of Convict Prisons since 1869 and was appointed in 1877 as the first chairman of the Prison Commissioners. Under the new legislation the Prison Commission became responsible to the Home Secretary for the administation of all prisons in England and Wales.

Since its inception in 1850 there had been a significant military influence in the management of the convict system in England and Wales. The three chairman, Jebb, Henderson and du Cane, were all Royal Engineer officers. Many of the prison governors were appointed directly from service in the armed forces. Subsequent promotion, usually involving transfer to another establishment, followed a hierarchical structure. This model was continued after 1877 and many of the convict prison governors achieved speedy promotion in the expanded service.

This contrasted with arrangements in Scotland. A series of centralizing statutes dating from 1840 had culminated with legislation in 1877 which paralleled that in England and Wales. However, the administration of prisons in Scotland had very close links with other parts of the criminal justice system. In both the use of imprisonment and the administration of prisons there was a clear recognition of the need for strong links between the prison and the court. The General Board of Directors of Prisons in Scotland, which took office in 1839, included among its members the Lord Justice General, the Lord Justice Clerk, the Lord Advocate, the Solicitor General and the Dean of the Faculty of Advocates. The first chairman of the Prison Commissioners for Scotland was the Sheriff Principal of Perthshire.

The militarism which was a feature of the management of the prison system in England and Wales continued until very recently. It exerted considerable influence on the manner in which prisons were run. This was an informal feature of the system since the prison service was and remains an arm of civil government. In several other countries in the world the link between the prison system and the military is a formal one. All prison personnel carry military rank. In some instances staff move between the various arms of the military into and out of the prison system. Such an arrangement has a significant influence on how a prison service is managed.

The Prison Commission for Scotland was abolished in 1929 and the management of prisons was absorbed into the Scottish Home Department, which was part of the Scottish Office. The abolition of the Prison Commission in England and Wales was delayed by the onset of the Second World War. Legislation for the abolition of the Commission was introduced in what was to become the Criminal Justice Act 1961. The proposal attracted fierce opposition in the House of Commons, in the press and in other informed circles. The government stood alone in supporting the proposal. Once the legislation was enacted responsibility for the management of the prison system in England and Wales was taken over directly by the Home Office.

The scale of the problems which have faced the prison system in England and Wales in recent years has caused many people to look back with nostalgia to the good old days of the Commission, forgetting that it also came in for its share of criticism. None the less, much of the present argument has been measured. It has usually centred on the uncertain relationship between the central administration in the Home Office and local management in prisons.

This uncertainty, it has been argued, was in the first instance deliberately fostered by officials in Whitehall who objected to the autonomy of the Prison Commission and who sought unsuccessfully to bring it within the control of tradional bureaucracy.

> The confusion and loss of morale which have helped to bring the Prison Service to the brink of disaster were predicted as long ago as 1963 by opponents of Whitehall's successful attempts, made then and subsequently, to gain greater bureaucratic power over the prison system . . . The growth of bureaucracy followed moves by Whitehall Mandarins and Ministers, introduced with some deviousness against fierce criticism in and out of Parliament. Their purpose was the absorption of the old Prison Commission, set up in 1877 to be responsible for prisons, within the control of the Home Secretary.[6]

The purpose of the exercise was not so much to bring prisons within the control of the Home Secretary, since he had always held parliamentary accountability for them, but rather to bring them within the administrative control of the Home Office; to make the management of the prison service part of the mainstream civil service.

FACE TO FACE WITH THE MACHINE

In 1981 I was asked to take up a post in prison service headquarters in Edinburgh. I moved into a world which was quite alien to me and into a way of working which required a great deal of understanding. During my early years in the prison service I was aware that there was an organization which existed at a level wider than the individual prison but there was rarely any need to wonder how it operated or indeed how it related to the prison. One's letter of appointment came from 'prison service headquarters' as did the impersonal note which advised a member of staff that he or she was to be transferred from one part of the country to the other. One would occasionally be faced with requests for information about individual prisoners. Further than that, whatever it was went on in this central organization had no obvious relevance to the task of caring for people who were in prison.

At that time the headquarters of the Scottish Prison Service was housed in a red brick Edinburgh office block which bore more than a passing resemblance to a badly designed prison. A discreet plaque at the front door indicated that the building housed various branches of the Scottish Office: its Superannuation Division, the Architects' Branch of the Scottish Development Department and Prisons Division.

That plaque told a story about how the management of the prison system was viewed. At the time there were approximately 10,000 civil servants in the Scottish Office. Over 3,000 of them, mostly prison officers, worked in the prison service. There were five major departments in the Scottish Office. Each was divided into several divisions. One of the divisions within the Scottish Home and Health Department was responsible for the management of the prison service. The administrator who headed the division was known as Director of the Scottish Prison Service. He reported to an Under Secretary, who reported to the Secretary of the Department, who reported to the Permanent Under Secretary of State, who reported to the Secretary of State.

This lengthy chain existed despite the fact that the Director of the Prison Service had day-to-day responsibility for over 5,000 prisoners and 3,000 staff in twenty penal establishments, of some 150 staff in headquarters and of an annual budget of some £60 millions. In 1982 there was some fine tuning of these arrangement. The post of Director was upgraded in the administrative hierarchy. One link in the reporting chain was removed and prison service headquarters was expanded to include seven full divisions. A similar arrangement, multiplied by a factor of ten, existed for the management of the prison service in England and Wales where the headquarters structure was a department within the Home Office.

Traditionally administrators in the civil service are attracted to jobs which involve advising their political masters on matters of policy. In the normal course of events they are not required to manage large organizations. Indeed, any jobs which do involve direct management have tended to be considered less attractive by those administrators who are aiming for senior positions. This has in the past been true of posts in the central administration of the prison service.

Most administrators would spend a relatively short period in prison service management before moving back to a more traditional job. Those who stayed for any length of time were generally seen to have opted for a backwater. This arrangement did not lead to an easy relationship with those who worked in prisons and who were career prison staff. It also made it difficult to develop a long-term, coherent strategy for the management of the prison service.

The relationship between the prison service and the other arms of the criminal justice process was made more problematic by this arrangement. Contact was generally made through the other parts of the Home Office or the Scottish Office which had a monitoring or advisory role in respect, for example, of the police. Connections with the judiciary and the courts were even more tenuous. All of these arrangements left the prison service in an isolated position and subject to inconsistent direction. There were major and far-reaching consequences. Twenty years ago one commentator had this to say:

> In the first place, rather than emphasize the 'inevitability' of the last one hundred years or so of 'prison reform', it seems to me important in 1974 to recognize that they were very largely (though not entirely) a mistake, a blind alley into which the British Government wandered as much through short-sighted financial and political expediency as through any considered penal philosophy. [7]

When Woolf came to look at the prison service in the wake of the Manchester riot, he found it necessary to look also at the management of the service. The debate which followed centred not just on how best to treat prisoners but also on how best to manage the prison service.

INTRODUCING CHANGES

In 1987 changes were introduced to the management structure within prisons in Great Britain. These changes were aimed at changing a military-type structure, made up of senior staff and 'other ranks', to unified structure based on the management of different departments within each prison. This was followed up in

1990 with changes to the structure above establishment level in England and Wales. [8] The former division of the country into four regions was replaced by one with fifteen areas. Three directorates were set up in headquarters in London, each of which had combined responsibility for some policy matters and for the management of a number of areas. A major criticism of the previous regional structure had been that it separated decisions on matters of policy from those on operational matters. The hope was that the new arrangement would bridge that divide.

The tension, at times destructive, between central and local management and between management and staff had been recogized by a series of official reports, many of which made suggestions for improvement. Earl Mountbatten made specific reference to this in his report into prison escapes and security. [9] In 1979 the report of the May Committee of Inquiry into the prison services in the United Kingdom [10] had this to say:

> That something has gone wrong with the relations between staff and local and central management is undeniable – evidence of distrust, alienation and suspicion occurred too frequently for the reality of that to be seriously in doubt.

In 1990 Lord Justice Woolf [11] reviewed the various managerial changes which had taken place in the prison service in England and Wales in recent years and found that they had

> done nothing to reduce this deep-felt sense of dissatisfaction. In many establishments there is a strong feeling of distrust of Headquarters.

In 1991 Sir Raymond Lygo was asked by the Home Secretary to carry out yet another management review of the prison service in England and Wales. In his report [12] he commented that

> The Prison Service is the most complex organization I have encountered and its problems some of the most intractable.

The Lygo Report is a curious mixture which advocates the

introduction of more efficient business practices to the prison service alongside a return to a more military model. It identified four key issues which needed attention. It reiterated Lord Justice Woolf's call for more visible leadership. It called for the prison service to be given a greater degree of managerial independence from the Home Office. It identified the harm done by divisions within the various parts of the prison service. It emphasized the need to clarify and reinforce the service's sense of purpose.

AGENCY STATUS

In 1988 the Prime Minister's Efficiency Unit published a report entitled 'Next Steps'[13] which was to have a far-reaching effect on the operation of many branches of the administrative civil service. This document recommended a radical restructuring of the way government business was carried out.

> The Central Civil Service should consist of a relatively small core engaged in the function of servicing Ministers and managing departments, who will be 'sponsors' of particular government policies and services. Responding to these departments will be a range of agencies employing their own staff, who may or may not have the status of Crown servants, and concentrating on the delivery of their particular service, with clearly defined responsibilities between the Secretary of State and the Permanent Secretary on the one hand and the Chairmen or Chief Executives of the agencies on the other.

It was not clear at the outset that the distinction between a small government department which would be responsible for policy making and a separate executive agency which would carry out that policy could be applied to the prison service. The review of the organization of the prison service in England and Wales which was completed in 1988 referred to the possibility of agency status for the prison service, commenting that such a concept had 'a particular resonance for the Prison Service because of its Prison Commission history'.

One of the main recommendations of the Lygo Report was that

the prison service in England and Wales should become an agency. This would separate it from the Home Office and allow it to operate with greater independence from day-to-day ministerial control. At the same time the Home Secretary would remain accountable to parliament for the prison service and would decide major policy matters. The Home Secretary accepted this recommendation and decided that the prison service in England and Wales would become an agency on 1 April 1993. The Secretary of State for Scotland set the same date for a similar change in the prison service in Scotland.

One of the first practical consequences came as a result of the decision to accept another of Lygo's recommendations, that the post of Chief Executive of the new agency should be filled by open competition. The Director General at the time, who was an administrative civil servant like his predecessors, had been in post since August 1991. He was generally reckoned to have done a good job, particularly in respect of giving visible leadership to the service in the wake of the Woolf Report and in promoting a sense of value for the work of the service. It was known that he had applied for what was in effect his own job. Following a protracted period of uncertainty the Home Secretary announced in December 1992 that the new Director General of the prison service in England and Wales and Chief Executive designate was to be a businessman who had previously worked for the Ford Motor Company, Granada PLC and as a television executive.

The prison service in England and Wales was launched as an agency on 1 April 1993. At the same time it published details of how it would operate. A Framework Document set out the respective responsibilities of ministers and of the Chief Executive as well as arrangements for finance, planning and management of personnel. It set out the prison service's statement of purpose, vision and goals. It defined the values of the service as integrity, commitment by and to staff, care for prisoners, equality of opportunity, innovation and improvement. The document listed the six goals of the service:

- To keep prisoners in custody.
- To maintain order, control, discipline and a safe environment.
- To provide decent conditions for prisoners and meet their needs, including health care.

- To provide positive regimes which help prisoners address their offending behaviour and allow them as full and responsible a life as possible.
- To help prisoners prepare for their return to the community.
- To deliver prison services using the resources provided by Parliament with maximum efficiency.

A Corporate Plan described the strategy which was to be implemented in the three years up to March 1996. This identified five key themes:

- Implementing further reforms arising from the White Paper 'Custody, Care and Justice'.
- Improving the performance of directly managed prisons.
- Increasing private sector involvement in the running of prisons.
- Delegating more responsibility to governors and transforming the relationship between headquarters and establishments.
- Using accommodation more effectively.

A Business Plan dealt with proposals for the first financial year of the agency's existence. This set what were described as 'key performance indicators' to measure progress towards each of the long-term goals.

PUBLIC SERVICE AND MARKET VALUES

The issue of involving the private sector in the management of prisons has been the focus of public debate for some years and has seen a change of direction. Speaking in July 1987 the then Home Secretary told the House of Commons that he could see no case

> for auctioning or privatizing the prisons or handing over the business of keeping prisoners safe to anyone other than Government servants.[14]

In July 1988 the same Home Secretary published a Green Paper which considered the options for private sector involvement in providing and operating centres for remand prisoners and for escorting prisoners to and from court.[15] Speaking in the House of Commons on 1 March 1988 Douglas Hurd made reference to the government's responsibility for the proper treatment of prisoners. However, he went on,

> I do not believe that these issues should stand in the way of attaining the practical benefits that private sector involvement may bring.[16]

When the Criminal Justice Bill was introduced to parliament in 1991 it contained provision for contracting out the management of new remand prisons. During the course of its passage an amendment was introduced which gave the Secretary of State authority to contract out the management of any prison.

The political path which had led to such a radical change of opinion has been described elsewhere.[17] The developments of recent years have brought a whole new set of concepts to the management of the prison service in England and Wales; market testing, contracting out and privatization.

According to the prison service,[18] market testing involves:

- Systematically analysing the work that needs to be done for the organization to meet its objectives.
- Specifying what needs to be done and to what standard.
- Opening this work up to competitive tender.
- Comparing the in-house bid with competing bids from outside tenderers to decide which will give the best value for money for the required quality of service.

The most publicized example of market testing at the time of writing has been the arrangement made for the management of the rebuilt Strangeways Prison in Manchester. This was put out to competitive tender. The Home Secretary agreed that existing management and staff could bid for the contract to run the prison. This process extended from October 1992 until July 1993 when it was announced that the in-house bid had been successful. A five-year service level agreement was entered into.

Another option which has recently been introduced is that of contracting out the management of different parts of the prison service to private contractors. This can take different forms, ranging from the management of a complete prison to the management of discrete parts of a prison, such as catering or health care services.

The provision of education services in prisons has been contracted out to local authorities for many years. Following the enactment of the Further and Higher Education Act 1992 the prison service in England and Wales had to seek tenders for this work. The saga of how this was done makes a sorry tale. It left many teachers who had worked with great commitment in prisons for many years facing months of uncertainty ending with the possibility of redundancy. Tenders for the provision of education services have now been let for all prisons in England and Wales. It remains to be proved that the new arrangements will lead to an improvement in the service provided or to greater efficiencies.

In many respects the principle behind contracting out certain services in a prison is a sound one. One of the structural weaknesses of the prison system in the past has been that it has tried to operate prisons as total institutions. Many of the services which are available in the community have been replicated within a prison. In some instances the result has been to emphasize the insularity of the prison system from society and to provide a service which has been viewed by many commentators as inadequate.

Considerable criticism has been levelled over the years at the provision of health care for prisoners in England and Wales. Until recently this was provided almost entirely in house. The prison service had its own permanent doctors, assisted by ancillary staff. Primary care was usually provided by prison officers who had received basic training in health care and who were known as hospital officers. In recent years the emphasis has changed and prisoners now have considerably more access to the National Health Service, in respect of both primary health care and of specialist services. This ensures that prisoners are likely to have access to a medical service which is equal in quality to that available to other members of the community. It also minimizes their sense of isolation from society. As far as the prison service is concerned it means that there is much less likely to be criticism of its care for the health of prisoners.

The greatest debate has been generated by the determination of the government of the United Kingdom to contract out the management of entire prisons. The most telling arguments against contracting out the management of prisons are based on an issue of principle. Briefly stated, this is that only the state, acting on behalf of society and through the courts, has the right to deprive a person of his or her liberty. Having decided that a person is to be deprived of liberty the state does not then have the right to contract the execution of that punishment to a private individual or company. A related objection in principle is that such private concerns manage prisons primarily as a means of making profit. The concept of making financial profit by depriving a human being of his or her liberty is held to be morally unacceptable. The contrary argument is that the state retains ultimate responsibility for men and women who are in prison and that it makes little difference in principle whether the state looks after them by means of a prison service which is directly managed or one which is contracted out.

When announcing in September 1993 his intention that initially 10 per cent of the prisons in England would be managed by private companies, Michael Howard, the Home Secretary, suggested that private enterprise would bring 'the benefits of better value for money and more innovative and imaginative ideas' to the management of prisons. This is the strongest practical argument advanced in favour of the contracting out of prison management. It is that the system of management by an arm of central government has resulted in a tired management style, wasteful of resources and with no incentive to be effective and efficient. Prison service management has failed to carry staff with it. They, so the argument goes, have turned instead to their trade union, the Prison Officers' Association, which has been obstructive and self-serving in reacting to any attempts to improve the prison service.

If the prison service is to become an efficient and well-managed organization it has to find a balance between protecting the public by keeping people sent to it by the courts safely locked up, giving prisoners an incentive to lead purposeful and law-abiding lives and managing all its resources in the most efficient way. Advocates of contracting out suggest that the prison service has failed to achieve these objectives because of its monopoly position and that the objectives will only be achieved if there is a healthy competition between the private and the public sector. The political argument is that there is nothing qualitatively different between managing prisons, coal mines, schools, railways, hospitals, or electricity stations.

The argument has not yet been taken to its logical conclusion with the suggestion that either the prison system or individual prisons should be fully privatized. At present in England and Wales the Home Secretary through the prison service acts as a servant of the court in carrying out its decision to deprive a person of his or her liberty. Privatization would mean that a private company would contract directly with the court to carry out this service and would lock up prisoners under the supervisison of staff and in a prison for both of which they were completely responsible.

Andrew Rutherford has summarized the matter of private involvement in prisons in the following manner:[19]

> Furthermore, presenting the problem in terms of prison management misses the core issue. There is significant room for improvements in the management of British prisons, but it does not follow that they would result from privatization. Indeed, there is every reason to suppose that existing difficulties would become more intractable. The management of prisons is inherently part of the public service. The reforms that are required largely concern areas outside the prison system, affected by decisions that determine the extent and distribution of punishment. These are exclusively policy issues, and it is in this domain that they must be addressed.

THE PRISON SYSTEM AS PART OF THE CRIMINAL JUSTICE PROCESS

The debate about how prisons should be managed is of topical and political interest in the United Kingdom at present. This question does not, however, tackle the more fundamental issue of what prisons are for and how the prison system should achieve its purpose. The sole reason for the existence of the prison in a democratic society is to execute the decision of the court that a person should be deprived of his or her liberty. In other words, the prison is an integral part of the criminal justice process.

A judge may have different reasons for deciding to send each individual to prison. The most common ones are that the person needs to be locked up for the safety of the public, that he needs to be punished, or to deter that individual or other potential offenders from future crime.

It is generally accepted that it is no function of a prison system to impose punishment on a person beyond that which is inherent in the deprivation of liberty. The comment of Sir Alexander Paterson, a famous English Prison Commissioner in the early part of the twentieth century, is frequently quoted on this subject:

> It must, however, be clear from the outset to all concerned that it is the sentence of imprisonment, and not the treatment accorded in prison, that constitutes the punishment. Men come to prison as a punishment, not for punishment. It is the length of the sentence that measures the degree of punishment and not the conditions under which it is served. It is therefore possible to have considerable variety in prison treatment without disregarding the basic fact that a prison sentence is still used by the Courts as a form of punishment.[20]

In a well-publicized judgement in 1982 (Raymond v. Honey) Lord Wilberforce expressed the same principle in legal terms, judging that a prisoner 'retains all civil rights which are not taken away expressly or by necessary implication'.

What this means, in a word, is that a court sends to prison those people who have to be deprived of their liberty. Once these people arrive in prison they should be treated with decency and encouraged to become law-abiding citizens. This notion underlies the statement of purpose which has been formulated by the Prison Service of England and Wales:

> Her Majesty's Prison Service serves the public by keeping in custody those committed by the courts.
> Our duty is to look after them with humanity and help them lead law-abiding and useful lives in custody and after release.

There is no great disagreement about these matters. Nor can there be any objection to the aim of making the prison service more accountable and more efficient in managerial and financial terms. There are grounds for suggesting that some of the major difficulties which have faced the prison systems in the United Kingdom in recent years have arisen from the fact that the proper link between the prison and the rest of the criminal justice system has become blurred.

The central management of the prison service has been located in a central government department. In the case of England and Wales this has been the Home Office. This has led the service to concentrate on relationships with the rest of the civil service and to be very aware of political influences. Arguably this has been done at the expense of links with the rest of the criminal justice system. The fundamental link between the court and the prison has become increasingly tenuous over the years. One example of this is the discrepancy which has grown up between the length of sentence passed by the court and the actual time which a person spends in prison. In respect of what used to be known as remission, and of parole, decisions about the release of prisoners are made not by the judiciary but by administrators. In more general terms the administration of the prison service in the United Kingdom is more closely linked to the administration of the civil service than to the administration of justice.

The first recommendation in the Woolf report on prisons identifies the need for greater cooperation among the various elements of the criminal justice system. Woolf made that recommendation after a thorough investigation of the strengths and weaknesses of the prison service. The fact that his first recommendation relates to the need for strong links between the prison service and the other branches of the criminal justice system is no coincidence. The reality that this linkage has not been as strong as it should have been has certainly weakened the ability of the service to cope with the difficulties which it has faced.

International comparisons in this respect are helpful. In many countries the administration of the prison system lies within the Ministry of Justice. This has the benefit of ensuring that all aspects of the criminal justice system can be coordinated while at the same time safeguarding the operational independence of each element, such as the judiciary. In the totalitarian systems of eastern Europe and the former Soviet Union the management of the prison system was usually to be found within the Ministry of the Interior. In many of these countries it has now been relocated in the Ministry of Justice.

As a variation on this arrangement, in some countries all services which deal with offenders come under one jurisdiction. These will normally include probation, prison and parole. This means that a proper balance can be maintained between care and supervision of the offender in the community and in custody. It also provides for a more efficient use of the resources which are available for these purposes.

LOCAL ACCOUNTABILITY

We have already established that the machine which is the prison service has no right of existence on its own. It is tied inextricably to the criminal justice system. Going further than that, one can say that in any country imprisonment only exists because society wishes it to do so. One can imagine a society in which there would be no imprisonment. Such societies have existed. The existence of the prison in many countries can be traced directly to former colonial influences.

In a democratic society it is important that this link between prison and the community on whose behalf it operates is recognized and maintained. In Western societies the modern notion of imprisonment owes much to the principle of exiling troublesome members from their communities. This concept has led many people to be ambivalent about imprisonment. On the one hand there is a demand that people who commit particularly serious offences should be locked away. On the other hand there is concern about the way people are treated when they are in prison.

In some respects prison is one of the last great secretive institutions in our society. We do not want to know what goes on behind its high walls. Yet at the same time we are curious to learn about this secret world. The truth is that not only does society have a right to know what goes on within its prisons, it has an obligation to learn about what is done in its name.

This principle can find practical expression in several ways. Each prison in England and Wales has a Board of Visitors. This is a group of independent men and women from all walks of life whose main function is to be a watchdog body, ensuring that the prison is managed in a decent and humane manner in accordance with the statutory rules and regulations. The Board has no executive power but it can be an important influence on how a prison is run. It has the right of direct access to the Home Secretary and to make public comment on any matter relating to the prison. How effective Boards are in practice is open to debate. The fact that members are appointed by the Home Secretary does place a question over their absolute independence. None the less, they have the potential to be influential representatives of the local community.

The community also shows an interest in its prisons through the involvement of many statutory and voluntary agencies who work inside prisons or who assist prisoners on release.

One might argue that there is a role for the local community, through its elected local authority, to manage prisons. Some form of central provision would probably have to be made for those prisoners who need to be held in conditions of maximum security. If all other prisons were managed directly on behalf of the community, prison would be less a place of exile, prisoners would have more opportunity to maintain their links with the community from which they had come and to which they would return. Given the possibility of better structured support for prisoners on release, there would be an increased possibility that former prisoners would lead law-abiding lives.

Such an arrangement would be in line with the current political thrust in the United Kingdom towards less direct involvement by central government in the lives of citizens. It would be a modern expression of the position which existed before the middle of the nineteenth century without the abuses involved in that previous system. It might even eventually lead to a reduction in levels of crime within that community.

REFERENCES

1. McConville, S (1981), *A History of English Prison Administration, Vol 1: 1750–1877,* Routledge & Kegan Paul, London.
2. Report of the Select Committee of the House of Commons on Scottish Prisons (1826), HMSO, London.
3. Howard, J (1777), *The State of the Prisons in England and Wales,* Wm Eyres, Warrington.

4. Select Committee of the House of Commons on Penitentiary Houses (1812), HMSO, London. For a description of the discussion in the select committee, cf. McConville (1981).
5. McConville, S (1981), ibid.
6. Evans, P (1980), *Prison Crisis*, Geo Allen & Unwin, London.
7. McLachlan, N (1974), 'Penal Reform and Penal History' in Blom-Cooper, L (1974), *Progress and Penal Reform*, Oxford University Press, Oxford.
8. HM Prison Service (1988), Review of Organization and Location Above Establishment Level, PA Consulting Group, London.
9. Report of the Inquiry into Prison Escapes and Security (1966), HMSO, London, Cmnd 3175.
10. Report of the Committee of Inquiry into the United Kingdom Prison Services (1979), HMSO, London, Cmnd 7673.
11. Report of an Inquiry into Prison Disturbances 1990 (1991), HMSO, London, Cmnd 1456.
12. Report by Admiral Sir Raymond Lygo (1991), 'Management of the Prison Service', Home Office, London.
13. 'Improving Management in Government: The Next Steps' (1988), HMSO, London.
14. Hansard, House of Commons, 16 July 1987, col. 1299.
15. Private Sector Involvement in the Remand System (1988), HMSO, London.
16. Hansard, House of Commons, 1 March 1989, col. 277.
17. Stern, V *Bricks of Shame,* 1993 edition, Penguin, Middlesex.
18. Prison Service Briefing Number 52, August 1992.
19. Rutherford, A 'British Penal Policy and the Idea of Prison Privatization' in McDonald, D C (1990), *Private Prisons and the Public Interest,* Rutgers University Press, London.
20. Ruck, S K (1951), *Paterson on Prisons,* F. Muller Ltd, London.

TWELVE

A Personal Credo

This has been the story of a personal odyssey which began in Edinburgh Prison over twenty years ago and which has passed through Polmont Borstal, Shotts Prison, Greenock Prison, Peterhead Prison, back to Shotts Prison and which rests for the time being in Brixton Prison, south London. In its course it has witnessed terrible and frightening events. It has also observed examples of great bravery and of selflessness. It has taken me through happiness and pain, through monotony and excitement. It has touched the depths and the heights of human behaviour.

This book began with the question 'What does a prison governor do?' It ends with the question 'Why would one want to do a job like that?' The answer probably is that prisons are in some respects right at the core of our humanity. They present us with the terrible dilemma of how we deal with people who do not fit easily into the accepted norms of society. These people form a heterogeneous group. Some have committed heinous offences which cry out against humanity. Many are basically decent men and women who have made a mistake or a series of mistakes in their lives and have found the rest of us quite unforgiving. Others are people who have given up the unequal fight for survival and who are measured as failures. Each of them is an individual.

It is easy for the man or woman on top of the Clapham omnibus going past Brixton Prison to be judgemental about those who are behind its high walls, to conclude that they have forfeited all rights to decent and humane treatment, that they deserve everything they

A PERSONAL CREDO **209**

get. It is not so easy to take this position when one deals day and daily with the prisoner as a person. To some extent the prison is a microcosm of the conflicts which are within each of us. This may be why we are so ambivalent about imprisonment and the prisoner.

Many writers have suggested that the manner in which a society treats its prisoners is a good reflection of its very humanity. Dostoyevsky expressed this in *Crime and Punishment* as:

> The degree of civilization in a society can be judged by entering its prisons. [1]

Organized religion carries a great deal of responsibility for the kind of prisons we have today. Much of the barbarous treatment meted out to prisoners over the centuries has taken place in prisons which were nominally under the control of one or other religious group. The form of imprisonment which exists today has its roots squarely in the Christian religion.

Students of ecclesiastical architecture and those of penal history might usefully compare the hermitic cells of early monasticism, grouped around a central church building, with the Victorian prisons which are still in use today. These consist of tiers of rooms, also described as cells, grouped around what often remains the most impressive building in the establishment, the prison chapel.

The similarities between the monastery and the traditional prison went beyond that of architecture. Prisoners were to be separated from all negative influences. They were to have no communication with each other. They were to be subject to 'good influences': the habit of regular work, the Bible to read and frequent visits from the governor and the chaplain.

The personal reformation of the prisoner became all-important. It was to be measured by admission of guilt, by expiation and by a firm purpose of amendment. In a religious context these processes are only to be measured between God and the individual. In the context of the prison, they were to be measured by third parties, by those who administered the system.

The imposition of such a structure bore within it the seeds of its own failure. Technically, this personal reform on the part of the prisoner was described as rehabilitation. As applied traditionally in the prison system, this principle was at best patronizing and at worst arrogant. It included the assumption that it is possible for one group of human beings to impose personal change on another human group.

Rehabilitation, properly understood, involves putting on again the garb of citizenship. This is not a strait-jacket into which one can be forced. It is a cloak which must be donned freely. One can and must be assisted in putting it on, but in the final analysis one must freely choose to do so. The need for this distinction is now being recognized by those who work on behalf of society in the prison system.

Those of us who work within the prison system have continually to struggle against the seduction that, because we wear a different kind of uniform from the prisoners, we are better people than they are. The reality of power within relationships, which is present in so many aspects of our daily lives, is to be found expressed with starkest clarity in a prison. Staff have control over every last detail of how a prisoner lives his or her daily life, often even to the extent of deciding when they may exercise their bodily functions. We have to remind ourselves continually that this power over what a person does cannot extend to power over the person him- or herself.

This distinction between power over what a person does and power over the person is an important one. It is a distinction which all of us who are in so-called positions of power in our professional lives must never forget. We must never succumb to the illusion that power to direct or even to control the actions of another person implies power over who the other person is, with the unspoken assumption that we can somehow force the other to change as a person. To be seduced in that way is to threaten our own freedom.

The part of my life in prison which has been the most far-reaching influence on my outlook was undoubtedly the time I spent as governor of Peterhead Prison. In 1988 it was a completely coercive environment. The consequences of this official response to the violence of the prisoners was predictable. The prisoners were not reformed, far less were they rehabilitated. Instead their behaviour became even more extreme. They took a perverse pride in showing that, although staff might have power over every last detail of their daily lives, they were able stubbornly to refuse to cede power over themselves as persons. No matter how coercive the regime, the power which the system had over individuals could not be absolute.

One prisoner who was in Peterhead throughout the 1980s has written about his feelings while he was there:

You do not touch me. There is nothing you can do to me that you have not already done. I am me and I am stronger and more powerful than you. You are nothing but an evil, sadistic cypher in a weak and powerless system. Surround me by time. Surround me with your stick-carrying screws. Move me from cell to cell twice every day. Put another gate in front of my steel door. Surround me with cameras. Be as you are – weak, frightened, powerless. Now there is nothing left you can do to me. You cannot make me any harder, any more dangerous, nor any more loathing. I hold in contempt your sadistic, weak powerlessness. All you have to offer me as an alternative to the freedom of having nothing else to lose is a light at the end of a 23-year tunnel – is the suffering of time. The only penance for my crimes you have the imagination to conjure up is time behind a door. [2]

Real change in behaviour only began when the system recognized the need to treat prisoners as individuals, to show a limited but increasing trust in them as responsible people. This was a high-risk strategy in an environment where trust was regarded as softness, where respect was seen as an expression of weakness. There was always a sense of unease, of fear about what the next day might bring, both on the part of the staff and of the prisoners. But gradually staff and prisoners came to recognize that a way of living decently together had to be found. This could not come about through an expression of power or coercion.

The prison system, to a greater extent than other large organizations, is a child of its own history. Its roots are to be found in the ambivalence which society has always felt towards those of its members who do not observe the rules and regulations imposed by the majority. This ambivalence has traditionally been expressed in a wish for an unusual combination of punishment and reformation. Since the abolition of capital punishment, imprisonment has remained as the ultimate mark of disapproval which society can inflict on one of its members. As such, it carries with it great symbolism.

The symbol of the scapegoat is well known in Judaeo-Christian tradition. The unfortunate animal was sent out into the desert to wander and eventually to die, bearing with it the guilt of the community. The principle of exiling individual men and women from their communities is not far removed from this notion. This was the punishment which was inflicted on Cain, who was sentenced to wander the earth after killing his brother. The custom of imprisoning offenders behind the high walls of a prison is a modern expression of the principle of exile. The manner in which we treat offenders also has a parallel with the scapegoat of the Old Testament.

The notion of prison as a place of exile may be convenient but it is no longer acceptable. If society takes on itself the right to punish people by depriving them of their liberty, it must also accept the obligation to welcome back those who have paid their debt. Our attitude to those who have broken the laws of society, who have forfeited the right to be members of our community, goes to the root of human emotion.

We have to recognize and to accept the prison as an integral part of the community. Yet much of society's attitude to the prison shows that the notion of exile is still very much alive. The high walls of the prison are intended to keep the community outside just as much as to keep prisoners inside. There are fine words in the Woolf Report about the need to develop the notion of the community prison and to encourage the prison system to build up links with all relevant sectors of its local community. By and large there is a recognition within the prison system that this is necessary.

But it has to be a two-way process. The community and its members have to accept the responsibility which they have for the prisoner and the prison. The criminal who has broken the law and who is sent to prison, for however long or short a period, remains a member of the community, while he or she is in prison. Unlike the biblical scapegoat, the vast majority of prisoners will return to the community on completion of sentence. The community has an obligation to prepare both the prisoner and itself for that return.

Society should not look to the prison to cure it of its ills. In the summer of 1993 the English tabloid press gave a great deal of coverage to the story of a boy in the northeast of England who had taken to petty crime and to eking out a living in the basements of high-rise flats in the housing scheme where he had been brought up. He was dubbed 'the rat boy' in some newspapers. At some point one journalist decided to seek out the mother of the young boy. She gave the journalist a telling quote, 'He's not a rat: he's my son.' In our society there is probably a better than even chance that sooner or later a boy such as this will end up in our prison system. When he does, the prison will be expected to achieve success where all other agencies have failed.

Reading of this young man one cannot help but think of John Steele, another former prisoner of Peterhead, who has written his autobiography.[3] There is a certain inevitability in Steele's story about the institutional road down which he passed. A road which began with severe beatings from his father, beatings which he could not understand, which proceeded through his time in an assessment centre, to approved school, to remand unit, to borstal, to Barlinnie Prison and to Peterhead Prison. The prison system was unable to cope with John Steele by traditional means. But that failure must be seen in the context of how society had already decided that he was a failure long before he came into the prison system.

His father had decided from an early age that he was a failure. School and his teachers quickly labelled him as a failure. The church labelled him a failure. The police labelled him a failure. And in due course he failed even in his criminality.

That is not to justify or to condone the crimes which Steele committed along the way. Yet reading his autobiography one is struck by the realization that at several key junctures in his life it should have been possible to stop his escalating spiral of failure. This did not happen and he ended up being treated as one of the most dangerous men in Scotland, locked in the dark box which was the punishment cell in Peterhead Prison, lying in the corner, covered in a blanket and his own excrement, crying to himself. 'I felt like a terrified child. I wanted to cry out. I wanted Ma. I wanted to die.'

Eventually the spiral was stopped when he was transferred to the Special Unit at Barlinnie Prison, where for the first time he was shown a degree of trust – and responded to it. After some years he was transferred to a minimum security prison. He was released in March 1992, having served the whole of his sentence.

The experience of imprisonment is not always negative. If it were none of us would have survived the length of time we have. There is frequently humour in prison, even if it is often macabre. Like the church visitor who was visiting during recreation time and was invited by a prisoner to play table tennis. The visitor refused, saying, 'I'm no good. You'll probably murder me.' As soon as he said it, he realized that the remark was inappropriate in the circumstances. Quick as a flash, the prisoner said, 'No, I won't. I'm in for robbery. But,' pointing to another prisoner, 'he might.'

From time to time in prison one comes across instances where the basic goodness of the human spirit shines through. It may be the older prisoner who takes aside the young tearaway, whom he sees about to repeat the mistakes which he himself made twenty years before, and convinces him that there is an alternative to beating one's head against the system. It may be the member of staff who gives a mentally disturbed prisoner the care and attention he needs. It may be the group of prisoners who entertain senior citizens or mentally disabled people at Christmas. After one such event I remember a young prisoner saying that for the first time in his life he had realized that there were people in the world who would appreciate his help and to whom he had something to offer.

Helping prisoners to think of others is a great challenge. It can be realized in many ways. In Brixton Prison there are no organized worksheds. Means of keeping prisoners occupied have to be found wherever they are available. Some prisoners spend their time making wooden items to be sold to help local charities. Others spend their time doing humdrum but essential work for a charity involved in cancer relief. This work has saved the charity thousands of pounds and has given the prisoners a sense of doing something which is worthwhile.

The experience of imprisonment will only be positive if it occurs within a just environment. Prisons must be and must be seen to be places where justice is the guiding star. If there is to be any hope that people who leave prison will be more law-abiding than they were before they were sentenced, the experience of imprisonment must impress on them the importance of justice. To have any hope of this, the actions of all those within the system, management, staff and prisoners, must be based on a recognition of the right which each has to expect justice in dealings with the other. Justice is not always easy to achieve in prisons, where the environment does not lend itself to respect for the person. It must be in the mind of the governor who hears the case against a prisoner accused of an assault on staff; it must be in the mind of the officer who is sworn at by the prisoner; it must be in the mind of the prisoner who is continually subjected to petty discipline.

The need continually to examine our actions and our motives extends beyond those who work in prisons to central administrators, to politicians, to interested commentators and to society at large.

Coming towards the end of his time as a prisoner, and indeed to the end of his life, Dietrich Bonhoeffer wrote:

> We have been silent witnesses of evil deeds; we have been drenched by many storms; we have learnt the arts of equivocation and pretence; experience has made us suspicious of others and kept us from being truthful and open; intolerable conflicts have worn us down and even made us cynical. Are we still of any use? What we shall need is not geniuses or cynics, or misanthropes, or clever tacticians, but plain, honest, straightforward men.[4]

If I have learned anything over the last twenty years, it is that complex problems do not have simple solutions. It is naive to divide our society into those who are good, who usually happen to be those who are in charge, and those who are bad. It is extremely difficult sometimes to recognize the humanity which is in everyone despite the terrible and stupid things which some people do. There must be a great temptation for those in public life to respond superficially to what are fundamental issues about human nature; to look for quick fixes.

In a Christian context it is worth remembering that when Christ said, 'When I was in prison you visited me' he did not make any conditions. He did not say, 'When I was *innocent* in prison you visited me.' And the only person who was ever promised entry to paradise was a convicted thief.

REFERENCES

1. Dostoyevsky, F (1991), *Crime and Punishment*, Penguin, London.
2. McGrath, J (1992), *Scottish Child*, June/July 1992.
3. Steele, J (1992), *The Bird That Never Flew*, Sinclair-Stevenson, London.
4. Bosanquet, M (1968), *The Life and Death of Dietrich Bonhoeffer*, Hodder and Stoughton, London.

Index

alcohol 33–35
'association' 36

Barlinnie 78,110,178,214
Board of Visitors 184f
borstal 20, 55, 63f
Brebner, William 16
Brixton prison 40, 46, 113–33, 209
bullying 68

Cambridge research 50f
chaplains 80
Chief Inspector of Prisons 25, 40,
    68, 113, 190
    for Scotland 16, 25
Chiswick Report 67
community, links with 117–76, 213,
    215
community prisons 174
complaints procedure 183
Cornton Vale 45
Crawford, William 15
Criminal Justice Acts 66, 67, 192,
    196, 200
criminal justice system 1595, 203ff
Custody and Care 88
Custody, Care and Justice 186

daily routine 78f
Dartmoor prison 150, 175
death in prison 67, 125–29

dehumanization 28, 59
deterrence 20
du Cane, Edward 137, 191

Edinburgh prison 4, 8, 26f, 29, 31,
    35, 45, 193
education 79, 165, 201
European Prison Rules 116
execution 12
exercise 79

families 30, 47, 81, 130f, 170–74
Feltham 67–70, 72
food 2, 32, 165
foreign prisons 1, 12, 13, 21, 22,
    23, 42, 47f, 51f, 71, 127, 144f
Fox, Lionel 19

Gladstone Committee on
    Prisons 17, 55, 137, 149, 154
Glasgow prison 16
Glen Parva 70
Glenochil 67, 71, 83
Gloucester 14
Greenock prison 45, 70, 75–83

'halls' 26
Hill, Frederic 16
hobbies 33
Holloway prison 46, 51, 121
Home Office 25, 178, *passim*